Marshall

W9-AGO-031

PICTURE CREDITS
Cover photo: © Sharon Smith/Bruce Coleman Inc.
AFP: 5, 40 • alt.TYPE/REUTERS: 14, 106, 112 • Bes Stock: 1 • J. Butchofsky-Houser/Houserstock: 64
• Camera Press: 28, 117 • Corbis Inc.: 46, 51, 53, 90 • David Cumming/Eye Ubiquitous: 32 • Embassy
of the Republic of Hungary (Singapore): 37 • Richard Esbenshade: 20, 38, 39, 41, 43, 45, 58, 62, 65,
69, 70, 74, 75, 77, 80, 83, 92, 94, 102, 103, 108, 113, 121, 124, 126, 127, 129 • HBL Network Photo
Agency: 36, 49, 50 • Dave G. Houser/Houserstock: 84, 120 • Hulton-Deutsch Collection: 23, 29, 31,
96, 115 • Image Bank: 4, 15, 82, 116 • International Photobank: 6, 55 • James Davis Worldwide: 76
• John R. Jones: 16 • Life File Photo Library: 7, 8, 9, 11, 13, 18, 22, 56, 66, 67, 79, 86, 89, 101, 125,
128 • Keith Mundy: 5 • STOCKFOOD/FRANK WIEDER: 130 • STOCKFOOD/EISING: 131 • Liba
Taylor: 73, 91, 105 • Travel Ink Ltd: 104

ACKNOWLEDGMENTS
Thanks to Holly Case of the Department of History at Cornell University for her expert reading
of this manuscript.

PRECEDING PAGE
Three generations of a Hungarian family dressed in their finest traditional clothes.

Marshall Cavendish Benchmark
99 White Plains Road
Tarrytown, NY 10591
Website: www.marshallcavendish.us

© Times Media Private Limited 1996, 1994
© Marshall Cavendish International (Asia) Private Limited 2005
All rights reserved. First edition 1994. Second edition 2005.

® "Cultures of the World" is a registered trademark of Marshall Cavendish Corporation.

Originated and designed by Times Editions
An imprint of Marshall Cavendish International (Asia) Private Limited
A member of Times Publishing Limited

Library of Congress Cataloging-in-Publication Data
Esbenshade, Richard S.
    Hungary / by Richard S. Esbenshade.— 2nd ed.
        p. cm. — (Cultures of the world)
    Summary: "Explores the geography, history, government, economy, people, and culture of
        Hungary"—Provided by publisher.
    Includes bibliographical references and index.
    ISBN 0-7614-1846-6
    1. Hungary—Juvenile literature. 2. Hungary. I. Title. II. Series: Cultures of the world (2nd ed.)
DB906.E83 2005
943.9—dc22   2004027454

Printed in China

7 6 5 4 3 2 1

CULTURES OF THE WORLD®

HUNGARY

Richard S. Esbenshade

BENCHMARK BOOKS

MARSHALL CAVENDISH
NEW YORK

CONTENTS

**Hungarians are proud of
their distinctive Magyar
features and strive to
preserve their cultural
heritage.**

The real charm of Hungary reveals itself in the quiet little cobbled streets where merchants display their wares for sale on the sidewalks.

INTRODUCTION

HUNGARY'S LONG AND EXCITING HISTORY began in the Ural Mountains. From there, the first Magyars migrated to the Carpathian Basin in Central Europe. Their Asian origin has bequeathed Hungarians with a unique culture and language, which they greatly value. Their literary and artistic traditions show a passionate commitment to their culture. Hungary's culture and history put it in a unique position to form a bridge between West and East.

Hungarians hope that the end of Communism has finally freed them to find genuine democracy, independence, and economic well-being. Two important steps have been taken—joining the North Atlantic Treaty Organization (NATO) in 1999 and joining the European Union (EU) in 2004. Hungary's transition to a market economy is one of the most successful among Eastern Europe's former Communist states. *Cultures of the World: Hungary* provides an insight into the resilience of the Hungarian people amid tumultous change and a history of adversity.

GEOGRAPHY

SITUATED IN THE LOW-LYING CARPATHIAN BASIN between the Alps and the Carpathian Mountains, Hungary has often been threatened by conquering armies from East and West. In times of peace, traders and travelers have brought new political ideas and fostered cultural innovation.

From the Middle Ages until World War I, the kingdom of Hungary extended from the snowy peaks of the Carpathian Mountains to the shores of the Adriatic Sea. However, with the 1920 Treaty of Trianon that concluded the war, Hungary lost over 70 percent of its territory, leaving a small, flat, landlocked country. Although this loss caused the Hungarian people much soul-searching, present-day Hungary—characterized by plains, fields, rivers, and lakes—retains its distinctive charms.

Opposite: **The Széchenyi chain bridge spans the Danube at Hungary's capital, Budapest. The river is a vital waterway for transporting goods and people between Budapest and other major European cities.**

Below: **Transdanubia, between the Danube and the Austrian border, is still an agricultural region despite the presence of many mining operations.**

A FLAT COUNTRY

One advantage of having a flat land surface is that Hungary is almost self-sufficient in food production and even exports such commodities as corn and beets.

Although Hungary is usually described as an Eastern European country, it is actually located near the geographical center of Europe. Hungarians like to think of themselves as Central European, an integral part of the continent and its culture. The country is 35,919 square miles (93,030 square km) in area, roughly the size of Indiana. It is about 328 miles (528 km) from west to east and 166 miles (267 km) from north to south. The Danube river in the northwest, the Ipel in the north, and the Mur and Drava rivers in the southwest form part of Hungary's borders. Hungary's neighbors are Austria to the west, Slovakia to the north, Ukraine and Romania to the east, and Serbia, Croatia, and Slovenia (all formerly Yugoslavia) to the south and southwest. Political changes since 1989 may have altered the names and identities of Hungary's neighbors, but have left its borders intact.

Hungary lies in a geographic formation called the "middle Danube depression." Dominated by one of Europe's largest plains, about two-thirds of the area is almost completely flat and less than 650 feet (198 km) in elevation. Hungary retains some small mountain ranges, but its highest peak, Mount Kékes, is only 3,327 feet (1,014 m) high. Nevertheless, Hungarians have managed to put more than half of their land area under cultivation—more than twice the European average.

What lies below the earth is also noteworthy. In Hungary the temperature underground increases by one degree every 59 feet (18 m)

in depth, one-and-a-half times that of the world average. This thermal activity explains the presence of the numerous mineral springs that have been used for centuries for bathing and therapy. The earth also yields substantial mineral resources: coal, magnesium, uranium, copper, lead, zinc, and large amounts of bauxite, which is used in making aluminum.

The warm and sunny days of summer bring out large numbers of sunbathers who lie down on any sunny, grassy spot.

CLIMATE

Hungary lies at the intersection of three major climatic zones: the Atlantic coast climate is mild and oceanic; the Mediterranean climate brings rainy winters and hot, dry summers; and the extreme Asiatic climate blows dry winds in from the Russian steppes. This means that Hungary's climate varies from year to year, as one or the other of these influences predominates. Temperatures can range from -4°F to 104°F (-20°C to 40°C), with the annual mean at 50°F (10°C). Average rainfall per year is 26 inches (66 cm), generally higher in the western part of the country, but that is also unpredictable.

THE MUTILATED MOTHERLAND

Hungarians, regardless of their social class or political stance, were deeply shocked and hurt by the loss of over two-thirds of their country's territory in the Paris peace settlement following World War I. Some 3.5 million of their fellow Magyars—one-third of the total population—found themselves residents of neighboring countries. In succeeding decades, the slogan "Small Hungary, no country; Big Hungary, heaven!" became a nationalist rallying cry. Although Hitler rewarded Hungary for being Germany's ally by restoring much of the lost territories in 1938, 1940, and 1941, these were taken away at the end of World War II, as Hungary once more was on the losing side.

Even today, Hungarians retain a strong feeling for these areas and the ethnic Hungarians who continue to live there: some 600,000 in Slovakia, 200,000 in Ukraine, 1.7 to 2.5 million (depending on who is counting) in Transylvania (Romania), and 500,000 in Serbia. They still use the old Hungarian names for the territories and their towns: Felvidék (FEL-vee-dayk), or upper country, for Slovakia, Erdély (AIR-day) for Transylvania, Délvidék (DAYL-vee-dayk), or southern country, for northern Serbia, and Vajdaság (VAI-dah-shaahg) for Voivodina, another term for northern Serbia. Despite these emotional ties, most Hungarians recognize political realities and do not support border changes. Neighboring countries that were once quick to accuse Hungarians of wanting their old lands back are now less worried that their ethnic Hungarian minorities would break away to rejoin their former homeland.

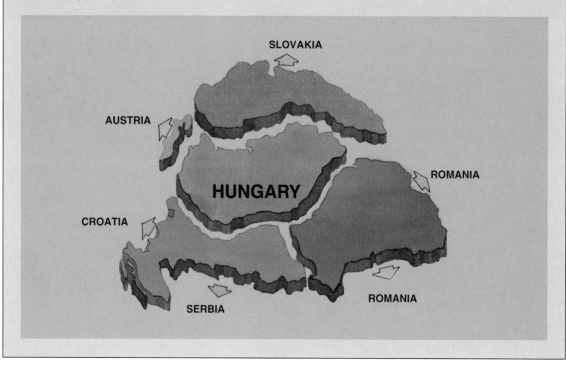

THE GREAT HUNGARIAN PLAIN

To the east of the Danube river stretches the *puszta* (POO-stah), a vast, apparently empty flatland that forms the heart of Hungary, both physically and spiritually. Like the expanses of the American Midwest, beneath the seeming emptiness lie both wealth and character. When the original Magyar tribes swept into the Hungarian Basin in the ninth century, they found this area of wild grassland ideal for shepherding and horse breeding, their traditional activities. After these semi-nomadic peoples decided to settle down, they planted vineyards and fruit trees, and so began the gradual transformation of barren land into a Central European breadbasket. The driving of huge cattle herds to far-off towns in Italy, Germany, and Austria was gradually replaced by a feudal system of agricultural estates, and the *csikós* (CHEE-kohsh), the Hungarian cowboy, was replaced by landowning nobles and their peasant serfs.

Much of the Great Hungarian Plain (Alföld) is under cultivation, livestock is fenced in, and the only remnants of the *csikós* are those who perform for foreign tourists. But parts of the *puszta*, especially around Hortobágy, retain an elusive, almost mystical charm: subtle coloration, delicate natural balance, sudden and violent changes in weather, the *délibáb* (DAY-lee-bahb) or Hungarian mirage, and man-made landmarks such as the *gémeskút* (GAY-mesh-koot) or *shadoof*, a kind of water-drawing apparatus in the shape of a cross.

The landscape of the *puszta* is punctuated by flocks of white sheep tended by shepherds who still wear traditional costume.

11

RIVERS AND LAKES

Hungary is defined geographically by rivers and lakes. The river systems of the Danube, or Duna (DOO-nah) in Hungarian, and the Tisza (TEE-sah) spread out over much of Hungary's territory. Irrigation provided by these two rivers has turned barren grasslands into fertile farmland. The western geographical region, between the Danube and the Austrian border, is called Transdanubia—"across the Danube." The other two main regions are the Great Plain and the Northern Uplands. The area east of the Tisza has traditionally been referred to as Tiszántúl (TEE-sahn-tool), "on the far side of the Tisza." In the past, seasonal flooding by the rivers and their tributaries put much of the surrounding countryside at constant risk of destruction. Flood control measures have now been put in place and there is less risk of flooding.

Hungary's lakes are dominated by Lake Balaton, the largest lake in Central Europe; the other main lakes are Lake Velence and Lake Fertő (most of which extends into Austria, where it is called Neusiedler See). Located about halfway between the Danube and the country's western border, and about one hour from the capital, Lake Balaton is easily accessible to tourists from Western Europe; over one-third of Hungary's tourist revenue comes from Balaton. Covering a surface area of 230 square miles (596 square km), Lake Balaton is very shallow, averaging only 10 feet (3 m) deep, with a maximum depth of 36 feet (11 m); the surface freezes completely nearly every winter. The lake has been called a "surrogate sea" for landlocked Hungary, as it moderates temperatures and affects rainfall. In addition to recreational resorts, Balaton's environs harbor unique wetlands, some of which are protected nature reserves for birds. But industrial development, sewage disposal, acid rain, and the draining of the Little Balaton marsh have endangered the Balaton environment.

"On the bottom step that from the wharf descends I sat, and watched a melon-rind float by. I hardly heard, wrapped in my destined ends, To surface chat the silent depth reply. As if it flowed from my own heart in spate. Wise was the Danube, turbulent and great."

—*Attila József,* By the Danube *(1936), translated by Vernon Watkins*

THE BLUE DANUBE

Most Westerners think of Austria when they hear about the romantic Danube, but it is in Hungary that the river is perhaps most beautiful. The Danube and its eight bridges form the very heart of Budapest. The river cuts the city in two and provides a majestic panorama, which has been declared an international cultural treasure by UNESCO. In the Danube Bend area north of Budapest, where the river takes its great turn to the south, spectacular fortifications, islands, and historic towns can be seen on both banks. The river also provides a major navigational route suitable for ocean-going vessels from Budapest south to Belgrade, in Serbia, and then east through Romania and Bulgaria to its mouth in the Black Sea.

From Budapest to the Serbian border, the river takes a slow-moving, gradual course. But this moderation is deceptive: the Danube has often spawned destructive flooding. Ice plugs can develop when the ice begins to break up but is restrained by the still-frozen river downstream. The river

then bursts through the "plugs" in a powerful barrage of water and ice; such an occurrence wiped out most of the capital (then still three separate cities) in 1838. In 1879, the seasonal second or "green" flood (green because the ice has melted, in contrast to the earlier wintry "white" flood) swelled the Danube to the point where it could not absorb the Tisza's waters, causing a backup on the Tisza that flooded and destroyed the historic city of Szeged. More recently, in 2001, the Tisza and its tributaries rose to record levels, adversely affecting over 25,000 people. The next year the Danube rose to a record high and flooded several areas. But in 2003 the Danube went the other extreme and was at its lowest level in over a century. It was the worst drought since 1950 and it led to the suspension of shipping services and wiped out 20 percent of the year's harvest.

Hungary is home to a large population of red deer, including these standing in the flooded forest of the Danube-Dráva National Park during the flood of 2002.

FLORA AND FAUNA

About 2,200 plant species and 45,000 animal species can be found in the undulating lowlands, low hills, grassy plains, rivers, and forests of Hungary.

Twelve percent of Hungary is covered by meadows and pastures, and 18.7 percent is covered by forests (mainly deciduous). Due to the fertility of its soil, about two-thirds of Hungary is used for agriculture, and the remaining 15 percent serves for infrastructure, mining, industry, the military, and domestic use. As a result, native plant cover is rare. A few remaining sites include Lake Baláta in Somogy, the marshlands of the Nyírség region, and the chestnut forests of Koszeg. Mixed beech, evergreen, oak, and, less often, pine forests cover the slopes, while acacia groves can be spotted on the Great Plain and western lowlands. Almond, medlar, and fig trees also grow in some places.

Large numbers of deer, wild boar, elk, and fox live in Hungary's forests. Hungary's wild boar is unusual. It is born brown in color with light stripes, but as it grows older, the stripes disappear and the whole coat becomes a uniform dark brown or black. Rabbits, partridge, quail, wild duck, and pheasant can be found in the lower regions.

Hungary's diverse habitats make it one of the best places to bird-watch in Europe. The great bustard, aquatic warbler, corncrake, ferruginous duck, and imperial eagle are just some of the globally threatened species that can be spotted in their natural habitat in Hungary. Large osprey nesting sites also can be seen along the Danube-Dráva rivers. Hungary's rivers are also teeming with fish. The native carp, catfish, pike, bream, bullhead, pike-perch, and trout are some examples.

CAPITAL, TOWNS, AND VILLAGES

The Hungarian social landscape is dominated by Budapest. Originally three cities—Óbuda, Buda, and Pest—the capital was unified in 1873. It is home to 1.8 million residents, about 18 percent of Hungary's population, and another million enter the city every day to work or shop. This huge metropolis is a legacy of its days as a major city in the Austro-Hungarian empire. Hungary's second largest city, Debrecen, hardly compares to the sprawling capital. There are seven other cities with populations above 100,000, but most of Hungary's people live in smaller towns, villages, and industrial centers, and they are spread evenly throughout the country.

Early visitors to Hungary described a vast, Asiatic swampland with huge villages. With the development of agriculture, the system of the *tanya* (TAHN-yah)—a kind of plantation-estate, very isolated and home to the wretchedly poor farmhands who worked there—predominated. What remains to this day is the sharp contrast between urban and rural living, characterized by romanticization of the countryside by city dwellers on the one hand, and suspicion of the city by peasants on the other.

Budapest is the economic, political, and cultural center of Hungary. At night, the illuminated Chain Bridge casts a romantic glow on the Danube.

MÁTYÁS
1458   1490

MÁTYÁS KIRÁLY TUDÓSAI KÖRÉBEN.

HISTORY

HUNGARIANS SEE THEIR HISTORY as an unending series of tragedies. The country has for centuries been subject to domination, occupation, and devastation by neighboring powers. Still, they are proud of their more than 1,000-year-old nation, once one of the most advanced in Europe.

THE GREAT MIGRATION

In A.D. 895–896 the original seven Magyar (ethnic Hungarian) tribes, led by Árpád, crossed the rugged Carpathian passes into the Carpathian Basin, ending a migration that began in the Ural Mountains and crossed the Asian steppes. The land the Magyars found was once settled by Celtic, Germanic, and Turkic tribes, and was under Roman rule from 14 B.C. to A.D. 430. By the time the Magyars arrived, the land was populated mainly by Slavic tribes; these they conquered and enslaved, while continuing to raid far and wide to gather booty and slaves. Their success was partly due to their use of metal stirrups and framed saddles that allowed them to stand and shoot their arrows in any direction while riding at full speed. In 955, after a crushing defeat at the hands of German Emperor Otto I, they ceased to venture outside the Danube Basin area.

Opposite: **The statue of King Matthias (reigned 1458–90) at the Millennary Monument in Budapest's Heroes Square. Statues of other major Hungarian leaders, from Prince Árpád and his chieftains to King Stephen to Lajos Kossuth, appear in the semicircular colonnade, which along with the square, was built in 1896 to celebrate Hungary's 1,000th anniversary.**

Below: **The arrival of the Magyars is depicted in vivid colors by painter Mihály Munkácsy. This painting hangs on the wall of the Munkácsy room in the Hungarian Parliament.**

ST. STEPHEN'S CROWN

The Holy Crown of Hungary, with its double bands and bent cross (see page 81), has become a symbol of Hungarian nationalism. The upper section was sent by Pope Sylvester II to Stephen I for his coronation in A.D. 1000, but the lower section, a gift from the emperor of Byzantium, was added by Géza I around 1074. As the Hungarian kingdom expanded, royalty across Europe fought to possess it.

After the Ottomans took over Constantinople, renaming it Istanbul, and launched their offensives against Christian Europe, the crown came to represent the defense of the West and the sacrifice of Hungary in defending the West. Kept in the United States during the early years of Communist rule, the crown and its accessories were returned to Budapest to great fanfare in 1978. In recent years the royal regalia have become a potent symbol of nationalism on the rise.

THE FIRST HUNGARIAN STATE

After their defeat, the Magyars looked around for a favorable alliance. There was a growing rivalry between the Eastern Orthodox Church, based in Byzantium, and the Roman Catholic Church, based in Rome. Hungary's leader, Géza, chose to support Rome. With the crowning of his son Vajk as King István (Stephen) by the Pope on Christmas Day of the year 1000, Hungary aligned itself firmly with Western culture.

King Stephen I, the "first European among Hungarians," immediately set about converting his subjects, by force if necessary. His strong hand created a uniform state with an advanced legal code, and the many foreigners he brought into the country created the basis for a multiethnic society. He was made a saint after his death, and despite a messy succession struggle, the Hungarian kingdom was solidly grounded for the next five centuries.

THE GOLDEN AGE

Despite bloody struggles for the crown, the country continued to prosper. It benefited from its location astride East-West trade routes, which encouraged the immigration of skilled and enterprising foreign settlers, strengthening the multiethnic nature of the population.

Hungary's progress was abruptly halted by the devastating invasion of the Mongols, led by Batu Khan, in 1241. King Béla IV fled to the coast, and more than half of the population was exterminated. But the invaders retreated as suddenly as they had come, and the country was slowly reconstructed, eventually surpassing its former prosperity.

The Árpád dynasty died out in 1301. Charles Robert of the House of Anjou became king of Hungary in 1308, ushering in a Golden Age of peace and prosperity. He reasserted his kingly power over the landowning nobles, increased trade, and developed agriculture and mining—Hungary at that time produced one-third of Europe's gold. He also introduced a stable Hungarian currency—the gold forint. His successor Louis the Great expanded the territory, campaigned successfully against the Ottomans, and founded the first Hungarian university. By the end of the 14th century, Hungary contained 49 cities, over 500 towns, and 21,000 villages, with a population of some three million.

Matthias Corvinus Hunyadi reigned from 1458-1490, bringing the full flower of the Italian Renaissance to the country. He invited great thinkers from Florence to share their knowledge, supported Hungarian literature, and built up a library, called Corvina, to rival the greatest of Europe. His reign brought economic prosperity, but taxes were raised to foster artistic growth and to form Hungary's first permanent professional military, called the Black Army. His 1486 Code of Laws put Hungary at the forefront of European legal progress, and earned him the epithet "Matthias the Just."

"The Mongol invasion is said to have been preceded by a number of menacing omens, including ravaging wolfpacks, unusual numbers of deformed newborns, and, finally, a solar eclipse. The invasion itself left 'nothing to be found back in our land, except the bones and skulls of those murdered and destroyed walls of our cities, still red from the blood so freely shed.' "

—Iván Völgyes, political scientist

OTTOMAN AND HABSBURG OCCUPATION

From the middle of the 14th century, the Ottoman Turks started attacking the Balkan states. The Turks defeated Hungary in 1526 when the army of Sultan Suleiman I killed King Louis II. Hungary was partitioned. Central Hungary, including the Great Plain and part of Transdanubia, came under direct Ottoman rule; the rest of Transdanubia in the west and the northern Carpathian area was controlled by the Habsburgs. Only Transylvania in the east was granted some independence as a principality under Ottoman suzerainty.

The Ottomans savagely exploited the land and enslaved the people. The Habsburgs were hardly less cruel: discriminatory tariffs and the preservation of a feudal landholding system kept Hungary poor and backward, and maintained it as a source of cheap raw materials for their growing empire. Constant war between the two powers on Hungarian soil also left the country devastated.

Transylvania became the symbol of the survival of the Hungarian spirit and the preservation of its culture. Many Transylvanian princes struggled for the reunification and liberation of Hungary. The 17th century was filled with Hungarian independence struggles. The most successful was by the *kuruc* (KOO-roots), or cross, which aimed to end Habsburg control of Hungary. The *kuruc* army, which took on the character of a peasant rebellion as well as national liberation, succeeded in occupying Upper Hungary and part of Austria. Subsequently, under the hero Ferenc

Arabic writing above a baptismal font shows the strong Turkish influence in a church in Pécs.

20

Rákóczi II, it posed a serious threat to the Habsburg court before being forced to surrender in 1711.

After the failure of the Rákóczi Rebellion, Hungary reconciled itself to Habsburg rule. Empress Maria Theresa developed the devastated country, building roads and schools, and draining the marshlands; but she did not support industry, introduce land reform, or allow the reunification of Transylvania with Hungary proper. She centralized the government and favored Latin over Hungarian as the language of governance. The situation of the peasantry, oppressed by both imperial rule and Hungarian landlords, worsened with the growing demand for grain in Western Europe. When Maria Theresa's successor, Joseph II, tried to initiate rational economic and governmental reforms in the guise of an "enlightened absolutism," the Hungarian nobles resisted. Joseph relented, and instead of modernization, sought the greatest economic benefit for the empire from taxing the feudal estate system.

"The Hungarian nobles, who keep you in servitude, do not consider you as citizens, but treat you as slaves. … Whatever grows on the fields, thanks to your toil and sweat, belongs to them. … What is left for you is serfdom and misery. … There is no other way but to exterminate the nobility—or give satisfaction by offering your blood and eternal servitude to our most insolent enemies …"

—György Dózsa, leader of the 1514 Rebellion

JÁNOS HUNYADI AND THE *DÉLI HARANGSZÓ*

János Hunyadi, a 15th-century Hungarian noble and soldier, and father of future king Matthias, gained fame throughout Europe as the "scourge of the Turks" for his success in battle against the Ottoman Empire. His finest hour came when he led his forces to meet a massive Turkish army at Nándorfehérvár (now Belgrade in Serbia). Pope Calixtus III, calling Hungary the "shield of Christianity," issued a Papal Bull (an order given by the Pope) decreeing that the bells of every Catholic church be rung daily at noon for a Christian victory. The battle ended in a crushing defeat for the Turks. The noon bell-ringing at churches, which Hungarians call *déli harangszó* (DAY-lee HAH-rahng-soh), continues to this day in parts of the Christian world, in honor of Hunyadi's 1456 victory.

THE DÓZSA REBELLION

In 1514, following a papal call to organize a crusade against the Turks, an army was recruited from among Hungary's peasants, who joined up in great numbers, in part because of religious fervor, but even more to escape their cruel lot on the landlords' estates. The landlords, needing their labor—the call occurred just at harvest time—and fearing that the army would turn against them, began using force to prevent their serfs from joining. This in turn aroused the peasants even more against their masters. Led by a Transylvanian lower nobleman named György Dózsa, they declared a "crusade" against the "wicked nobility" and began destroying the large estates.

The nobles raised an army of their own and, after four months, defeated Dózsa's large but ragged forces. Dózsa, the "peasant king," was forced to sit on a white-hot iron throne, with a glowing crown and scepter, and his starved followers were forced to eat his charred flesh before being killed in turn—a kind of violent retribution characteristic of Hungarian history. The nobles' revenge against the peasants took some 70,000 lives. As if this were not enough, the nobles passed legislation equating the Hungarian nation with only the free noble class, tying the peasantry to the land and depriving them of rights for all time. The sharp alienation of the peasantry from the ruling elite remained, to some degree, until recent times. Dózsa was glorified by the post-World War II Communist rulers, with statues in his honor and streets named after him in towns across Hungary.

At the Battle of Timisoara, the 1848 revolutionaries suffered a great defeat that made it impossible for them to continue their insurrection against the Austrian occupiers. (Timisoara is now a part of Romania.)

GROWTH OF NATIONAL CONSCIOUSNESS

In the 19th century nationalism spread across Europe. In Hungary, the national renaissance began with an exploration of the native Magyar contributions to Hungarian history. A class of intellectuals, drawn from the lower and middle nobility, favored the use of Hungarian over Latin and German. They were concerned about the social and economic development of the nation. By the time of the "First Reform Generation" of the 1830s, the rich landowners had begun to realize that Hungary's increasing backwardness and poverty were harming them too, and that reform was necessary for modernization.

The two most prominent Hungarian statesmen of the 19th century, Count István Széchenyi and Lajos Kossuth, both now celebrated as national heroes, are a study in contrasts. Széchenyi was a practical, realistic liberal reformer who dedicated himself to building and strengthening the country; he believed steady pressure on the government by an educated people was the most effective way to achieve reform. Kossuth was a national revolutionary with a romantic vision; he wanted to unleash the masses against the enemies of the nation. Széchenyi had grave misgivings about Kossuth's radical course, but it was Kossuth's Freedom Struggle of 1848 that eventually led to a short-lived Hungarian liberation.

REVOLUTION AND COMPROMISE

On March 15, 1848, the poet Sándor Petőfi recited a poem called *National Song* to a group of young men in a Pest-Buda (the capital's old name) café, setting off the Hungarian national revolution. The same day, Kossuth arrived in Vienna to meet with the emperor; he was granted his radical reforms, and a virtually independent Hungarian government was installed.

However, by the end of the year, the revolutionary tide had ebbed, and the Austrian rulers were ready to take their revenge. The powerful imperial army descended on Pest-Buda and smothered the new state. Kossuth and his followers retreated to eastern Hungary, and in a stunning turnaround, the Hungarian army drove out the Austrians from their capital. But at this point geopolitics intervened: the young Habsburg Emperor Franz Joseph I urgently requested assistance from Tsar Nicholas of Russia, and the huge Russian army marched in to put an end to the revolution. Hungary was subjected to a merciless and humiliating occupation. Kossuth fled the country and spent the rest of his long life in exile, agitating for Hungarian independence. Count Széchenyi, on the other hand, ended up in an mental asylum in Austria, where he committed suicide some years later.

By the 1860s, Austria's hold on Hungary had been weakened by passive resistance on the part of the Hungarians, tensions among other nationalities within the empire, and a weakening international position. The Hungarian statesman Ferenc Deák, a brilliant constitutionalist and indefatigable negotiator, pressed Emperor Franz Joseph for concessions. After the Prussian army defeated the Austrians in 1866, the emperor realized that, more than anything, he needed stability and peace at home, and the next year he agreed to the Compromise of 1867. The Compromise transformed the Habsburg Empire into an Austro-Hungarian monarchy—a dualistic state granting Hungary full sovereignty in conducting its internal affairs.

"The poverty and squalor were appalling. … The Turks had pushed Hungary back into the Middle Ages, the Austro-Christian liberators had pushed her back further still, but most fatal in keeping her backward was the attitude of the Hungarian nobles themselves."

—Paul Ignotus, writer

The Austro-Hungarian monarchy, with its sole ruler who was both King of Hungary and Emperor of Austria, lasted until the outbreak of World War I. Hungarian culture flourished, and a relatively liberal and democratic political order was established. Jews and other minorities were invited to adopt the Magyar language and culture, and thus be considered fully Hungarian and equal citizens. This 'generous' gesture was in effect forcible assimilation, and the minorities as a whole were excluded from political power. In addition, the nobles retained their privileged position, and the peasant masses remained in squalor and misery. But this was ignored in the whirl of progress: in 1896, the 1,000-year anniversary of the Magyar tribes' migration was celebrated with an exposition and the inauguration of the first subway line on the European continent, and the 'Second Reform Generation' developed plans to modernize the economic and political system.

THE POET-LIBERATOR

Sándor Petőfi was barely 25 years old when he inspired the March 15 uprising in Budapest. Petőfi joined the national army and was killed in battle against the invading Russians on July 31, 1849. (Other reports claimed he died a prisoner-of-war in Siberia.) He had a premonition of his fate, expressed in his poem *One Thought Torments Me*, which includes the lines: "Let me die on that battlefield. Let my young blood flow there from my heart. … And above my corpse wheezing horses will trot off to the well-deserved victory, leaving me trampled to death."

His poetry was lyrical and mixed romantic love with freedom and nationalistic feelings. Every young Hungarian knows his poem *Freedom, Love* by heart. Petőfi remains for many Hungarians a national hero and martyr.

WORLD WAR I

The outbreak of World War I put an abrupt end to the Austro-Hungarian monarchy's prosperity. Hungary entered the war on the side of the Central Powers and suffered a crushing defeat at the hands of the Allies.

In the chaos of wartime, movements for radical social and political change arose. At the end of the war, a bourgeois democratic revolution swept Count Mihály Károlyi into power in Budapest. However, he resigned soon after, and a Bolshevik regime headed by Béla Kun took over in March 1919. In the confusion, Czech, Romanian, and Serb troops occupied large parts of Hungary, with the Romanians capturing Budapest in August. Admiral Miklós Horthy's counter-revolutionary army finally restored order after the Romanians left in November. Horthy was appointed regent in place of a king in 1920.

Subsequently in 1920, the Treaty of Trianon deprived Hungary of two-thirds of its territory and more than 60 percent of its population. American President Woodrow Wilson's declaration of the self-determination of nations guaranteed the right of Czechs, Slovaks, Romanians, Serbs, and Croats to be joined with their new countries, but Hungarians felt that they were treated unfairly, since about one-third of Magyars along Hungary's borders were left in neighboring Czechoslovakia, Romania, and Yugoslavia for political or strategic reasons.

Exhausted and dejected, Hungarian troops return to Budapest from the front lines in 1918.

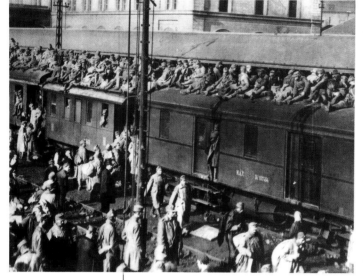

INTERWAR HUNGARY AND WORLD WAR II

In the early 1930s, young writers and students from the populist movement went to the countryside to investigate the wretched lifestyle of the peasants. They celebrated the peasants as the suffering "true Magyars" and called for radical land reform and social justice. In the capital, cosmopolitan writers agitated for a free press, a democratic government, and workers' rights. At the same time, growing anti-Semitic feelings (hatred of Jews) fed a growing fascist movement. The Horthy regime resisted the pressures from both left and right. However, when the Allies refused to help Hungary regain its lost territories, the country turned to Germany, which it believed would help in its quest.

These Hungarian troops near Budapest could do nothing to spare their capital: the city was badly damaged by both the German and the Soviet army.

Germany annexed Austria on March 12, 1938, and in September that year, Nazi leader Adolf Hitler got the other European powers to agree to his plan to annex part of Czechoslovakia. Hungary was rewarded for its support with the gift of most of the area it had lost to Czechoslovakia 18 years earlier. Hitler effected the return of Transylvania to Hungary in 1940, and the territories in Yugoslavia in 1941. In return, Hungary sent troops to fight with the Axis. Meanwhile, Hungary's leaders, realizing that Germany was losing the war, opened secret negotiations with the Allies. Hitler found out, and the German army occupied Hungary in March 1944 and installed the fascist Arrow Cross party in power. The Soviets invaded later that year and, after a destructive battle for Budapest, liberated Hungary on April 4, 1945.

Since many of the fighters in the 1956 Revolution were teenagers, they could not legally be executed until age 18, so they were kept in prison for two years or longer and then executed when they came of age.

FROM COMMUNISM TO INDEPENDENCE

Hungary's Communist leaders, led by Mátyás Rákosi, forced a Stalinist system on Hungary. They outlawed all associations and organizations they could not control. They introduced Soviet-style central planning and the production of consumer goods was neglected in favor of heavy industries. The population was terrorized, and prisons and labor camps were filled with opponents and those whose family background was "suspicious."

Soviet leader Joseph Stalin's death in 1953 created an atmosphere of reform and strict centralized control was relaxed. Mass anti-Soviet demonstrations in Poland in the first half of 1956 encouraged a similar demonstration by students in Budapest on October 23 that year. The rebellion soon spread throughout the country, and workers' councils took over the factories. Imre Nagy, a Communist who believed in a more human "Hungarian socialism," became prime minister and urged the rebel bands to lay down their arms, while trying to convince the Soviets that the situation could be resolved. Instead, the Soviet army invaded Hungary on November 4, crushing the rebellion and killing some 30,000 in Budapest alone. The Soviets placed János Kádár in power in return for his promise to do their bidding. Soviet reprisals included prison for more than 25,000 and the execution of 229, including Imre Nagy. Approximately 200,000 refugees left the country. Once again, Hungary lay devastated.

But Kádár was smart enough to know that the Stalinist era of total control of the people was over. He gave in to some of the demands of the revolutionaries, such as ending the drive to collectivize agriculture, while condemning the uprising itself as a "counter-revolution" led by "fascists and spies." While remaining a loyal subject of the Soviet Union, Kádár was able to liberalize the economic system in Hungary, provide people with a better standard of living and privileges such as owning a car or a vacation house, and the right to travel to the West (unheard of in the other Communist countries), and gain some autonomy for his country.

By the 1980s, Hungary appeared very liberal—it was known as the "happiest barracks in the Communist concentration camp." But much of the industrial reform was artificially constructed, unemployment concealed by three workers doing one man's job, the standard of living supported by money borrowed from abroad, and the government shortsighted and corrupt. After Soviet leader Mikhail Gorbachev began the changes in the Soviet system known as *glasnost* (transparency) and *perestroika* (restructuring), the leaders of the Eastern European countries, including Hungary, found it harder to resist similar changes themselves.

Kádár was removed from power, and the new government agreed to enter negotiations with the opposition groups, which resulted in an agreement to hold free, multiparty elections in early 1990 and to move to a market economy and a parliamentary democracy. In 1989 Hungary decided to allow thousands of refugees from East Germany to pass unhindered across its border into Austria, thus playing a major role in the fall of the Berlin Wall and the "Iron Curtain."

Hungary was proclaimed an independent republic on October 23, 1989. All governments since 1990 have moved toward full Euro-Atlantic integration: Hungary joined the North Atlantic Treaty Organization (NATO) in 1999 and became a member of the European Union (EU) in 2004.

In a symbolic gesture, Hungarians burn the portrait of Stalin to signify the end of the Communist era.

GOVERNMENT

HUNGARY HAS CHANGED ITS political system from one where a single party, the Hungarian Socialist Workers' Party, controlled every aspect of government to one in which different political parties, with different ideas and representing different constituencies, freely compete for the votes of citizens.

The road to democracy has not been easy. After more than 40 years of repressive Communist rule, the people are leaving behind a system of obeying leaders, believing official lies, and voting when told for new laws and structures of governance, which coexist alongside old habits and mindsets. Still, Hungary's big step from socialism to a multiparty democracy and the private ownership of property has occurred at an incredible pace and with comparative stability, a model for former communist regimes throughout Central and Eastern Europe.

Left: **The local town hall is the center of regional administration.**

Opposite: **The Parliament Building in Budapest is imposing and dominates the riverbank.**

GOVERNING HUNGARY

The current Constitution of the Republic of Hungary sets out European principles (the separation of powers, parliamentary democracy, and the universality of human rights) alongside Hungarian constitutional traditions.

Hungary's parliament is unicameral and consists of 386 members of parliament, elected to four-year terms. Parties must receive at least 5 percent of the country-wide vote to be represented in parliament. A legislative body with extensive lawmaking powers, the Hungarian Parliament created the institutional and legal framework for the rule of law and a market economy during the 1990–1994 parliamentary cycle. Frequent debates on policy and the setting up of investigative committees keeps parliament in check. Hungarian voters are allowed two votes: one to support a candidate in his constituency and the other to support a party list. Every Hungarian above 18 living in Hungary or residing there on election day is allowed to vote. Since 2004, Hungarians residing temporarily overseas but who have a permanent address in Hungary can also vote.

Most of the executive powers of government lie with the prime minister, elected by a simple majority vote by parliament. When the prime minister loses support, a "no confidence" motion is introduced and another prime minister is proposed in his place. The government consists of the prime minister, ministers of the 14 ministries, two ministers-without-portfolio, and the minister leading the Prime Minister's Office. Government members do not need to be members of parliament.

The president of Hungary acts as a guardian of the democratic process. As head of state, he plays an important role in the event of a national emergency and has the power to initiate or veto legislation, postpone or dissolve sessions of parliament, and set the date for parliamentary elections. But his authority requires a ministerial countersignature and he

Parliamentary delegates are elected in a complicated system involving both individual candidates and party lists (seats are allocated according to the support each party receives), as well as a "national list" meant to compensate for under-represented parties.

can be removed from office if he violates the constitution or other laws. The president of Hungary is elected by parliament in a secret ballot by a two-thirds majority for a 5-year term. Árpád Göncz was elected president for two terms (1990–2000). Ferenc Mádl is the current president.

Hungary is divided into the capital city Budapest, 23 districts of Budapest, 19 counties, 20 urban counties consisting of major cities, and villages. In contrast to a Soviet-type centrally controlled council, individual communities assert their right for representative democracy and self-government by electing a body of representatives and through local referendums. The rights of local governments include the right to own and regulate property, to earn income and levy taxes, and to issue local decrees. Local governments also maintain public roads and places, and provide basic social services and health care.

Hungarians casting their vote in the 1990 elections, the first free multi-party elections in nearly half a century.

The judicial courts of Hungary are an independent branch of the Hungarian state structure. Judicial recourse is considered a fundamental human right. Overseen by the National Council for Justice, justice is administered by the Supreme Court, the Court of Appeal, county (municipal) courts, and local (municipal district) courts. Judges must not be a member of any political party and cannot conduct any political activities.

Former Sports Minister Ferenc Gyurcsány took over as Hungary's prime minister from Péter Medgyessy on October 4, 2004.

POLITICAL PARTIES

Hungary's multiparty system took shape in the transition period of 1989–1990. In 1989 the Hungarian Socialist Workers' Party (MSZMP) renounced its monopoly on power and transformed itself into the social democratic, left-wing Hungarian Socialist Party (MSZP). Remaining communists continued to operate the dissolved party as the Workers' Party, but in elections held between 1990 and 2002 this party failed to obtain sufficient votes to be represented in Parliament. Pre-1949 political parties reorganized themselves and many new parties were formed in the late 1980s. In 1988 and 1989 respectively, the Independent Smallholders' Party (FKGP) and the Hungarian Social Democratic Party (MSZDP) reemerged. The rightist Hungarian Democratic Forum (MDF) was formed in 1987. Two liberal parties, the Alliance of Free Democrats (SZDSZ) and the Federation of Young Democrats (Fidesz), were formed in 1988.

After the first free elections in 1990, the government was formed by a coalition of Christian-conservative parties: the Hungarian Democratic Forum (MDF), Independent Smallholders' Party (FKGP), and the Christian Democratic People's Party (KDNP). The opposition parties consisted of the Alliance of Free Democrats (SZDSZ), Fidesz, and the Hungarian Socialist Party. József Antall, president of the MDF, was the prime minister of Hungary from 1990 until his death in 1993.

The same six parties were elected to parliament in 1994, except this time the Hungarian Socialist Party (MSZP) secured the majority of the vote, followed at a distance by the liberal Free Democrats (SZDSZ). Together, the MSZP and SZDSZ formed the government in a socialist-liberal coalition.

In 1995 Fidesz transformed itself from a liberal to a "civic" party and was renamed Fidesz-Hungarian Civic Party (Fidesz-MPP). In the 1998 elections, Fidesz-MPP won the most seats and formed a conservative, right-wing coalition government with the FKGP and the MDF. Viktor Orbán, president of Fidesz-MPP, was made prime minister. A new ultranationalist, extremist party, the Hungarian Justice and Life Party (MIÉP), received 3.63 percent of parliamentary seats.

Hungarians at a political rally at the Heroes' Square in Budapest during the 2002 elections.

The current socialist-liberal government was formed after the 2002 elections by the Hungarian Socialist Party (MSZP) and the liberal Alliance of Free Democrats (SZDSZ), while Fidesz-MPP and MDF formed the opposition. FKGP and MIÉP lost their seats in parliament. MSZP nominated Péter Medgyessy as their candidate for prime minister. In 2004 Medgyessy tried to dismiss the economy minister, who was from SZDSZ, but failed. The move made him unpopular with both the Socialists and their coalition partner, the SZDSZ. Medgyessy then resigned and was replaced as prime minister by the former sports minister, Socialist Ferenc Gyurcsány, on October 4, 2004.

Hungary can be said to have a pluralistic multiparty system and not just a united anti-Communist system. The range of the ideological stands of its political parties and the many different interest groups they represent have provided an environment of democratic competition. However, inter-party squabbling, rather than working together on political and economic reforms, has characterized Hungarian politics since 1990.

ECONOMY

AFTER MORE THAN 40 YEARS OF COMMUNISM, Hungary's economy has made a swift but painful transformation to capitalism. It is now one of the most advanced market economies in Central and Eastern Europe.

ECONOMIC INDICATORS

As a sign of the times, the private sector accounted for nearly 80 percent of Hungary's GDP in 2003, as compared to just 18 percent in 1989. More than 90 percent of prices are determined by the market. Exports to advanced economies have also increased from 27 percent (during the 1960s to the 1990s) to 84 percent in 2000. Inflation has also declined from 14 percent in 1998 to 4.7 percent in 2003. Foreign direct investments have poured in, more than $23 billion since 1989.

Nevertheless, this transition has not been smooth. More than one million jobs disappeared between 1989 and 1996, increasing the unemployment rate from 0.5 percent to 11.7 percent. This situation has since improved but unemployment is unevenly spread across the country; it is especially persistent in the underdeveloped eastern and northeastern regions. Hungary's per capita income also remains half that of the "Big Four" European nations (Germany, United Kingdom, France, and Italy).

Hungary's industries used to have a captive market locally and in the former socialist countries. In 1990, increasing imports and an end to government subsidies gave them a rude shock. Between 1989 and 1992 the volume of industrial production dropped by 44 percent, and the workforce was cut by 40 percent. The impact was felt most keenly by the engineering, metallurgy, manufacturing, mining, and building materials industries. Over the last decade, a focus on specialization has revived the engineering, vehicles manufacturing, telecom products, electric lights, chemical fibers, and clothing industries.

Above: **Hungary's farmers have had a tough time adapting to the loss of captive markets and government subsidies, increased taxes, and new international animal rearing regulations and food hygiene standards. Farmers would also be more productive if they had access to modern machinery.**

Opposite: **The Audi Hungaria Motor plant in Gyor is a symbol of Hungary's success in attracting vital foreign investments.**

41

CREATING THE "SOCIALIST ORANGE"

Communist idealists believed that it was possible to grow or produce everything the country needed. Thus Hungary had to produce steel and grow cotton and oranges so as not to depend on capitalist countries. The campaign for the "socialist orange" was supposed to prove socialism was the superior system. But Hungary is not Florida, and it proved impossible to actually grow oranges there. Still, this failure could not be admitted without throwing the whole system into question, so "criminals" responsible for the failure were found and punished, and the efforts continued.

THE COMMUNIST LEGACY

The Communists had a grand vision for the peasant country. Their goals were heavy industrialization, the creation of a large working class, and the collectivization of agriculture, turning farmers and farmhands into state employees. Under the principle that the country's resources belong to all the people, the state declared private ownership of land, shops, or factories illegal, and took away all property beyond personal belongings.

In the late 1960s, the Kádár regime placed an emphasis on industrial products, but the government allowed small private enterprises to be established, mostly shops, and later small restaurants and other food vendors appeared. In agriculture, members of state and collective farms were allowed to rent small plots to cultivate in their spare time and to keep the profits from their crops. The state was to concentrate on producing grain and livestock, which were more capital-intensive. As a result, food products became abundant. Recognizing the low income of its citizens, the government allowed Hungarians to take on a second job.

As the control of the economy by Party officials and central planning offices decreased, more and more transactions and exchanges took place outside the official economy between private citizens and even between factories, collective farms, and enterprises. This whole network of trading and services became known as the "second economy," as opposed to the official or "first" economy.

Nevertheless, the economy was in crisis. In 1988 the government instituted Hungary's first value-added and personal income taxes. People were working harder and harder, yet their standard of living was falling.

Appreciation money, respect money, hidden money, handshake money, honorarium, spreading money, sliding money.

—Hungarian euphemisms for "bribe"

STANDARD OF LIVING

The Communist system has left Hungarians with an infrastructure that is old, decaying, and substandard. Many apartment complexes, buildings, factories, and streets are in disrepair or even falling apart. Equipment in most manufacturing plants is outdated and inefficient.

The socialist legacy has, ironically, also left Hungarians with many inequalities in income, with urban dwellers being richer than the villagers and those without children being better off than those with families. Capitalism has not been kinder—60 percent of the population suffered a drop in income after 1990. The rich (managers of private businesses and state-owned companies and top government bureaucrats) have gotten richer and the poor (farmers, pensioners, homemakers, villagers, and the Roma) poorer. At the end of the 1990s, about two-thirds of the population still lived on a subsistence level.

The economy may be improving, but it is still hardly possible for many Hungarians, especially professionals and other "intellectual" workers in the state sector, to live on the salary from their primary job. Many must take on another job or freelance work, or do special projects to make ends meet.

Factory and manual workers begin work by 7:00 a.m. or earlier, and the official workday is over by 2:00 or 3:00 p.m. Offices start later, at 8:00 or even 9:00 a.m., but still usually close by 4:00 p.m. For all too many, the official "quitting time" is still seen as the time when "real" work, bringing in more money, begins.

Hungarian workers are hard-working and many take on second or third jobs in order to have a reasonable standard of living.

ENVIRONMENT

HUNGARY'S ENVIRONMENT HAS PAID THE PRICE for forced Stalinist-style industrialization in the past and the present swift transition into a market economy. Hungary's water system is contaminated by untreated sewage, runoff from fields treated with chemical fertilizers, and industrial waste. Toxic chemicals and jet fuel left by the Soviet army contaminate the soil, ground water, rivers, and lakes. Emissions from motor vehicles and electric plants pollute the air. Sulfur dioxide emissions from low-grade coal, still used for industry and domestic heating, lead to acid rain. Much of Hungary's population lives without adequate sewage systems, and many towns and villages rely on unsanitary water supplies.

The main concerns of the Hungarian government and people have been the economy, jobs, and social welfare rather than the environment or sustainable economic development. In 1998 only 1.1 percent of the country's GDP was spent on environmental protection and investment projects, less than in Slovakia, the Czech Republic, and Poland.

Although protection of the environment began in the 20th century, when the first Nature Protection Act was passed in 1910, Hungary's desire to join the European Union has helped make the environment a government priority. Hungary's parliament enacted the National Environmental Program in 1997, focusing on areas most important for EU membership. By 2001 spending on environmental projects had increased to about 1.5 percent of GDP, and by 2003 Hungary's legislature had adopted about 70 to 80 percent of EU environmental laws and regulations. Since the late 1990s, there has also been growing public awareness, with the help of nongovernmental organizations and the mass media, of the need for environmental protection. The main areas Hungary needs to improve on are waste management, energy efficiency, and pollution reduction.

Opposite: **Declared a UNESCO World Heritage Site in 1995, Aggtelek National Park's limestone hills and forest cover are ideal for walking, cycling, and bird-watching. But the park's true treasures lie below in the extensive cave systems, with their countless stalactites and stalagmites, and underground rivers, lakes, and waterfalls.**

WASTE MANAGEMENT

The disposal of hazardous waste is a major environmental problem in Hungary. Most waste is dumped into landfills, but in 2003, fewer than 100 landfills met EU environmental requirements. The remaining 2,500 are an environmental risk, especially to groundwater, and will have to be modernized or closed. Environmental damage caused when the Soviet army occupied Hungary has been estimated at US$1 billion. With international support, 20 out of the 171 contaminated military bases have been cleaned up, but activities have since slowed for lack of money.

Current waste collection and recycling is limited, because of a lack of money. In one year, Hungary can produce 3.9 million tons (3.5 million metric tons) of biodegradable organic waste, consisting of urban waste, agricultural residue, sewage sludge, and organic industrial waste. Of this, only 3 percent of solid urban waste is recycled, and as of 2004, there was no government plan for recycling household waste.

Hungary's largest hazardous waste incinerator in Dorog is owned by the French Onyx Group, which incinerates 30 percent of the hazardous waste. Some major industrial plants, pharmaceutical companies, and hospitals have constructed on-site incineration facilities. In general, the waste generated by industry is decreasing due to attempts to minimize waste and clean up production. Red mud, which until the mid-1990s was about one-third of all hazardous waste in Hungary, has been reduced with the decline in aluminum processing.

The government enacted a new waste management law in 2001 and is carrying out plans for the separation and composting of waste. It is also encouraging the introduction of low-waste technologies, the setting up of comprehensive waste treatment systems, manufacturers to be more responsible, and the reuse of products.

AIR POLLUTION

As of 2003, approximately 44 percent of the population lived in areas that did not comply with national air-quality standards. Vehicles are the biggest source of pollution, accounting for 50 percent of total emissions in 1995. Hungary's car population has tripled in the last 20 years to 2.5 million. Transportation policies add to the problem: the focus is on constructing new highways rather maintaining and upgrading existing roads, and subsidies support car manufacturers instead of more environmentally friendly forms, such as public transportation. Industry is the second largest air polluter. Many power plants are equipped with electrostatic precipitators, but not all are effective in reducing air pollution. The abundant use of domestic coal and lignite in homes, both high in sulfur, also pollutes the air with sulfur dioxide.

Technological improvements and new regulations in Hungary's energy sector, as well as the phasing out of coal-fired power plants, will mean cleaner air in the future.

Nevertheless, air quality has improved over the last decade as emission levels have declined. Carbon monoxide emissions, for example, dropped from 1.1 million tons (997,000 metric tons) in 1990 to 832,245 tons (755,000 metric tons) in 1999. This is the result of less industrial activity and increased technical improvements in the energy sector, which has also reduced emissions of particulates. Tighter vehicular regulations, such as requiring vehicles manufactured in or imported into the country to comply with strict EU emission regulations, and improvements in fuel quality have also reduced pollution. An energy plan issued in 1999 by the government proposes a gradual move toward cleaner technologies, including emission controls for the use of coal and the replacement of coal-fired power plants with gas turbines.

Water pollution is a big problem in Hungary. Industrial and domestic waste is dumped into waterways.

WATER POLLUTION

Hungary's rivers and lakes are very vulnerable, as 95 percent of Hungary's surface water supply comes from neighboring countries. Pollution from those countries can end up in Hungary. The cyanide spill in Romania in 2000 is a good example.

Half of Hungary's sewage is discharged without treatment. Only 20 percent of Budapest's wastewater is treated; the rest ends up in the Danube River. Sewage pollutes rivers and the soil and ground water along riverbanks. The dumping of industrial waste also pollutes the Danube and Tisza rivers. Agricultural activity adversely affects water quality when excess fertilizer washes into waterways or animal waste is disposed of indiscriminately.

The Municipal Wastewater Project for Hungary, started in 1999 and scheduled to finish in 2006, intends to reduce pollution in the Danube river basin and to improve wastewater operations and utilities. This project aims to expand and upgrade two wastewater treatment plants in Budapest and Dunaújváros and to construct more sewage systems for Budapest. Experts will also try to solve odor problems, study the feasibility of using sludge to reclaim slag deposits, and find new methods of treating wastewater. Hungary has signed every international water protection treaty and bilateral water-quality protection convention with its neighbors, as of 2002.

While over 95 percent of Hungarians have access to a water supply, in 2002 only 2 million homes were connected to the public sewage system, an issue the government is trying to resolve.

CYANIDE SPILL INTO THE SZAMOS, TISZA, AND DANUBE RIVERS

On February 1, 2000 a reservoir wall at the Baia Mare gold mine in northern Romania collapsed, releasing approximately 3.5 million cubic feet (100,000 cubic m) of cyanide, used to extract gold from waste, into the Szamos (Somes) river, and, later, the Tisza and Danube rivers. The cyanide destroyed wildlife and fish stocks (*right*) and affected the water supply of 2.5 million people in Central Europe. About 221 to 331 tons (200 to 300 metric tons) of dead fish were removed from these rivers.

This cyanide spill has been described as Europe's worst ecological disaster since the 1986 Chernobyl nuclear accident in Ukraine. The Tisza was officially declared a dead river and was expected to take at least five years to recover. Hungarian towns along the Tisza banned the use of water, fishing, and sale of fish—threatening the livelihoods of many fishermen. Emergency water supplies had to be brought in for those living by the rivers.

The Hungarian daily *Magyar Hirlap* reported crowds of stunned people gathering with black flags to "mourn" the river. Zoltan Illes, then the environmental spokesperson for parliament, warned: "The fact that heavy metals also got into the rivers means an even worse problem. It will poison the whole food chain."

If accidentally sold on the market and eaten, the poisoned fish would cause serious kidney, liver, and blood diseases. The region was then witnessing a tourism revival, according to the National Tourism Board, with 80 percent of the tourists coming to fish. However, in March 2000, local news reports said that the turnover of fishing produce had fallen by 80 percent nationwide. Local fish restaurants and hotels also went out of business.

Hungary, Romania, and Serbia demanded damages from the gold mine's owners, a joint Romanian–Australian company, Aurul S.A.

The good news is that cyanide breaks down in sunlight and dilutes quickly. Water-protection authorities have reported encouraging signs of recovery in the Tisza river. Tests made one month after the spill showed that plankton, which were completely wiped out, had almost returned to normal levels, providing food for any remaining fish. The Tisza's cyanide level had also dropped to what was considered safe. But it was unclear how much zinc, lead, and mercury, which may have long-term toxic effects, remain in the river bed. Many Hungarians, unconvinced that their river is safe, are still not drinking or washing with the riverwater.

NATIONAL PARKS

About 20 percent of Hungary's original woodland has been seriously damaged, due to aggressive agricultural cultivation and forestry, rapid industrialization in the 19th century, and environmental pollution. Shrinking natural habitats have led to the disappearance of the European bison, and the beaver, lynx, wolf, and auroch. Some 535 plants, 855 animal species, and all 3,600 caves are now protected. Protected flora include the Great Plain's wild peony, spring adonis, and sage; the forest cyclamen flower found in western Transdanubia, and the meadow anemone found in the Nyírség. Protected birds include the egret, bustard, plover, and avocet. Animals on Hungary's endangered list include the European mink, Bechstein's bat, Eurasian otter, European squirrel, and lesser mole rat. Fortunately, the threat to animal and plant species in Hungary is still not as high as in some West European countries.

Ten national parks, 36 landscape protection zones, and 142 nature protection areas, nearly 10 percent of the country, has been set aside to preserve Hungary's flora and fauna. The eleventh national park is in the east Nyírség region, on nearly 247,000 acres (100,000 hectares) of land.

Hungary's first and most famous national park and Central Europe's largest area of grassland (*puszta*) is Hortobágy National Park. Under protection since 1972, Hortobágy's total territory is 200,155 acres (81,000 hectares). It was listed as a World Heritage Site in 1999. Hortobágy has three landscapes: floodplain forests and ox-bow lakes, marshes and lakes, and the *puszta*. The Hortobágy Puszta is Hungary's most important seminomadic shepherding region and early Magyar domesticated animals—Hungarian gray cattle, the Hungarian *racka* (RAH-tskah) breed of sheep, and Hungarian horses and buffalo—roam freely here. The mirages on the arid *puszta* have been immortalized in Hungarian myth and legend.

Kiskunság National Park was founded in 1975 and spans an area of nearly 188,000 acres (76,000 hectares) between the Danube and the Tisza rivers. The Bócsa-Bugac sand dunes and *puszta* form the park's largest and most variable section with sandy forests, alkaline grasslands, dunes, natron lakes, marshes, meadows, and fields. Many species of indigenous Hungarian flora and fauna and traditional peasant farming methods and lifestyles still exist here.

More than 90 percent of Bükk National Park is covered by forest. Beneath the limestone Bükk Hills are 500–600 caves, which extend to a total of about 22 miles (35 km). Stone Age tools and fossils of flora dating back to the Ice Age have been discovered in them. This park is famous for its stepped waterfall, with a fall of 56 feet (17 m), along the Szalajka stream. The Aggtelek National Park is also known for its cave system.

Őrség National Park in southwest Hungary, opened in 2002, is home to 111 protected species of flora. Many traditional log-wall houses and U-shaped Őrség houses are found here here, as well as precious deer stocks and the breeding grounds for 45 species of fish.

A stalagmite column in Aggtelek National Park's caves.

Sixty percent of Hungary's birds are found in the Danube-Ipoly National Park in the north. Körös-Maros National Park, in the southwest, is a sanctuary for bustards. The Balaton National Park is a nestling site for about 250 bird species and is also the only place in Hungary where the lip fern can be found. The Danube-Dráva National Park hosts Hungary's largest osprey nesting site, the highly protected lesser tern, and the unique habitat of two native flowers: the royal fern and the shepherd's cress.

HUNGARIANS

HUNGARIANS SEE THEMSELVES as a small group of unique people who have struggled for many centuries to survive in the midst of other, often hostile, nations. They have a strong sense of national and ethnic pride, but are often insecure about their future and place in the world.

The Carpathian Basin has long been a melting pot for many ethnic groups, and relations between Hungarians and the minorities living in the country have ranged from uneasy to hostile. Among Hungarians there is traditionally a strong division between city dwellers and country people. Sometimes they have less in common with each other than with people of other ethnic groups living in the same town or in a neighboring village.

Left: **Two youngsters enjoy a ride on their grandfather's donkey.**

Opposite: **A Hungarian Romani wearing traditional clothes makes a living as a street musician.**

POPULATION FACTS AND FIGURES

An aging population is becoming a heavy burden for younger workers.

Hungary has a population of about 10 million, of which about 90 percent are ethnic Magyars. Approximately 18 percent live in Budapest, and another 47 percent in other cities and towns. The remainder live in rural areas, a relatively high percentage for Eastern Europe. Population density is 280 people per square mile (108 people per square kilometer), around the European average.

With a declining birth rate and lower life expectancy, Hungary's population has been in decline since the 1990s. The life expectancy of Hungarians, average 72, is one of the lowest in Eastern Europe, the result of high death rates for working-age males caused by from overwork, stress, unhealthy lifestyle and diet.

In 2004 the average number of children per family was 1.31 (estimate). The number of abortions is high, at about 70 percent of the number of births. High rates of divorce and unstable family structures have also contributed to the low birth rate.

As of 2001, about 4.5 to 5 million ethnic Hungarians lived abroad, most in neighboring countries, especially in Romania. Substantial numbers of Hungarians have also migrated to Western Europe, Australia, Canada, and the United States. Some 1.6 million Hungarians are in the United States. Many Hungarian Jews left the country during and after World War II, and over 200,000 Hungarians fled the Soviet occupation that crushed the uprising of 1956.

THE MAGYAR DISTINCTIVENESS

The Magyars took their name from the original seven tribes that settled in Hungary, the Megyers. Hungarians call themselves and their language "Magyar." The term *Magyar* is also used in English by social scientists to describe ethnic Hungarians. The word *Hungarian* comes from "Onogur," a Bulgarian-Turkish word meaning 10 arrows, referring to the alliance of 10 tribes—later seven—that decided to unite and move west into Hungary.

Hungarians pride themselves on their pure and distinctive ethnic heritage. They are usually said to have "Asiatic" facial and physical characteristics, although there has been so much mixing of peoples since the arrival of the Magyar tribes that they are now not much different, in a racial sense, from the peoples around them. What is clear is that the main source of Hungarians' distinctiveness is the preservation of their language over the centuries.

Hungarian is part of the Finno-Ugric family of languages, completely unrelated to any of the Slavic, Romance, or Germanic languages spoken in the surrounding countries. Hungarians see the preservation of their language and culture as a historic mission. St. Stephen's acceptance of Christianity and the later struggles against invading Mongols and Turks gave the Hungarians another mission, that of preserving Christianity and Western culture from, ironically, the "barbarians from the East," which the Magyars themselves had once been.

The debate among Hungarians over whether they are essentially "Eastern," and different from Europeans, or "Western," and fully a part of European culture and civilization, has become a major point of division in politics and culture. There is still no agreement over what it means to be Hungarian: nationalists accuse others of being "not Hungarian enough," and are in turn accused of being "not fully European."

"It can be said that Asia was the cradle of the Magyar, and this child of the East, who had been feeding on the breast of Asia for thousands of years, now came to learn in the schools of Europe."

—Ferenc Jankovich, writer

THE HUNGARIAN CHARACTER

The question of what is Hungarian was especially sensitive during the years of communism, when Party activists tried to turn Hungarians into "Soviet people." Expressions of national or cultural pride were condemned as "nationalist deviation." During the Kádár era, it became more acceptable to explore the national character. But different groups defined a "good Hungarian" in different or even opposing ways that often excluded other ethnic groups or political opponents from participating in the affairs of the nation.

Pride in being Hungarian leads to a great sensitivity about losing face. Hungarians have never forgotten the instances of national humiliation—the 1526 defeat by the Ottomans, the failure of the 1848 Revolution, or the partition of the country in 1920. And they are also very sensitive to everyday situations in which they might feel personally humiliated. The word *balek* (BAH-lehk) refers to someone who is

THE "MOST HUNGARIAN" HUNGARIANS

Hungarians have always felt an emotional connection with those people who were cut off from the country by the Trianon Treaty. This feeling was especially strong in the 1970s and 1980s, when there were reports of discrimination against Transylvanian Hungarians in neighboring Romania. Although Hungary was a less developed society, conditions for Hungarians outside Hungary often remained even more simple and traditional.

Some Hungarians in Transylvania and elsewhere still live in ethnically uniform villages, cut off from much of the developments of the modern world. They speak old forms of Hungarian and live simple, self-sufficient lives. These people are idealized by nationally-minded Hungarians as the "most Hungarian," in whom Hungarian culture can still be found in its "pure" form, unaffected by the consumer culture of the West. With Hungary becoming more integrated into Western Europe and the international consumer market, many Hungarians are traveling to ethnic Hungarian villages in Transylvania to find their "roots." It is ironic that they feel they must go beyond Hungary's borders to find the real Hungary.

cheated, and a *balek* often appears as the fool in Hungarian cartoons and television shows. Sometimes it seems that Hungarians are constantly watching out for people who might take advantage of them, making them the *balek*. They have a sense of themselves as victims and feel that others, especially those from the West, can never understand them. Hungarians feel they have contributed to and sacrificed much for the West, but are not appreciated as full members of the European or Western community. Yet, they also are insecure about whether their run-down and inefficient society and their Hungarian mentality actually deserve to rank with the rest of Europe, and they are likely to contrast things, such as the poor service in a restaurant, unreasonable bureaucratic procedures, or a messy room with "the way they do things in Europe."

But Hungarians can also be very generous to foreigners. They possess an old world elegance and politeness, and will go out of their way to help a stranger. They are hard-working and full of ambition and creative energy. They can be exuberant celebrants and can also be deeply moved by compassion or the tragedy of fate.

Opposite: **Hungarians from Transylvania are supposed to be more genuinely Hungarian than even those living in Hungary.**

Despite the difficulties besetting the Hungarian economy, this Angolan father and his four sons have found a better life in Hungary.

MINORITIES IN HUNGARY

Germans, Serbs, Slovaks, Romanians, and the Roma or gypsies make up most of the recognized minorities in Hungary today. They speak Hungarian as well as their mother tongue—the latter very badly, for most of them. The minority groups have been offered generous civil rights, in part because the Hungarians want to set an example for their neighbors in the treatment of their large Hungarian minorities.

Other minorities include 4,000 to 5,000 Greeks, whose ancestors first arrived in the 16th century. During the 1948 Greek civil war and the 1967 military coup d'état, thousands of Greeks settled in Budapest and other major Hungarian cities. There is also a small population of Africans, Arabs, and Asians, many of whom came during Communist times from small socialist states for study or work and remained. More recent has been the arrival of refugees escaping the turmoil in neighboring countries. Many of these are ethnic Hungarians, but they also include Romanians, Croatians, and a number of Bosnian Muslims from war-torn Bosnia-Herzegovina.

TWO SIGNIFICANT MINORITY GROUPS

JEWS Around 100,000 Jews in Hungary survived World War II, one of the highest figures in East Europe, and many took up prominent positions in the postwar Communist government in the hopes of preventing another rise in fascism. But this led many Hungarians to associate Jews with communism, although most of the leading dissidents, or opponents of communism, in the 1970s and 1980s were also of Jewish origin. Hungarians also remember the role that Jews played in the past: they formed a high proportion of the professional and merchant classes, filling positions that educated noble Hungarians were too proud to take. Thus, ironically, there are Hungarian stereotypes of both the "communist Jew" and of the "capitalist Jew." Now most Hungarian Jews are intellectuals and technical workers living in Budapest, are fully integrated into Hungarian social and political life, and feel as Hungarian as anyone. But old prejudices die hard, and anti-Semitism has reared its ugly head among the most extreme of Hungarian politicians since the fall of communism.

ROMA The Roma *(right)*, often called gypsies, migrated to Europe from India during the Middle Ages. Hungary is home to some 550,000 to 700,000 Roma, the largest of the minority groups. The Roma originally made their living as peddlers, tinkers, musicians, and in other door-to-door trades. Dramatic and romantic "Hungarian Gypsy music," such as *Piros Rózsák Beszélgetnek (“Red Roses Are Talking”)*, is the traditional accompaniment to a Hungarian restaurant meal. Although this music has always been and is still played by Roma musicians, it is actually not Roma in origin, but 19th-century European café music that the Roma have adapted and made their own. During the communist era, the Roma were forced to settle down, respect borders, and be registered with the authorities. In exchange, they were provided with stable housing and jobs in factories or on agricultural cooperatives. But prejudice against these darker-skinned people remained, and they were kept in the lowest-paying, dirtiest, and toughest jobs.

Hungary's Roma, along with those in other countries, are becoming more aware of their cultural identity. They have organized themselves into local, regional, and national associations, and since 1990, three Roma have served in parliament. In June 2004 Hungarian Livia Jaroka became the sole Roma legislator in Europe to be elected to the European Parliament.

SOCIAL DIVISIONS

After the Communist takeover, a substantial working class was created, made up of miners, steelworkers, bricklayers, machinists, and factory workers. Admission to high schools and universities, and positions in the Party and government administration, were determined by social class, giving worker and peasant families an advantage and creating a kind of equality never seen before. Peasants were pushed into large collective farms, producing an "agricultural proletariat" or rural working class.

Beginning in the 1960s, government concern with efficiency and production led to the creation of a class of technocrats—trained managers, engineers, and technicians who administered the factories and collective farms. At the same time, the *nomenklatura*, a class of officials in government and industry, took on more and more power at the local level and collected all possible privileges for itself.

A new middle class emerged in the 1970s and 1980s, when economic reforms allowed private farming as well as the operation of small private enterprises. After 1989 a free market gave a class of entrepreneurs and business people the chance to grow. The *nomenklatura* was able to transform itself from Communist officials into capitalist owners and managers, while keeping its ill-gotten wealth. The big losers in the transition are rural workers and blue-collar workers, whose factories are unprofitable and will likely have to close. The difficulties of changing the system have caused new social tensions and a growing gap between rich and poor.

One group that deserves special mention is the intellectuals, whose social and political role has been much larger in Eastern Europe than in the West. They have great ambition and creative energy that can help solve Hungary's problems, but they have always tended to speak for and about the masses of people without getting to know their feelings and desires.

Although entrepreneurs and managers have been successful in the new economic order, the majority of the population still belongs to the working class.

GENIUS IN EXILE

Many Hungarians have made a name for themselves in the international arena. Many achieved success while living abroad or were born overseas to Hungarian parents. Albert von Szent-Györgyi Nagyrapolt discovered Vitamin C, found in especially high quantities in Hungarian paprika; János Irinyi invented modern matches; Oszkár Asbóth was the first to invent the helicopter; Ányos Jedlik invented the electric motor, Ottó Titusz Bláthy the electrical transformer, and Albert Fonó the jet propulsion engine; Dr. Ignác Semmelweis's proposal to sterilize all instruments used in childbirth caused a dramatic drop in infant and maternal mortality in hospital deliveries.

In addition, Hungarians made discoveries that either laid the groundwork for or made possible the practical application of the phonograph (Farkas Kempelen's "speaking machine" paved the way for it); the telephone (Tivadar Puskás invented the telephone exchange, and established a "telephone newspaper"—the forerunner of today's electronic mail bulletin boards); the electric railway (Kálmán Kandó); and television (Mihály Dénes). Baron Lóránd Eötvös revolutionized physics in the late 19th and early 20th centuries with his discoveries. He is remembered by several laws of physics and units of measure that are named after him, and Albert Einstein declared Eötvös's discoveries to be a pillar of his work. In the United States, János (John) von Neuman has been called "the father of the computer:" he directed the Electronics Computer Project at Princeton that developed the modern computer. Hungarians Leo Szilárd, Eugene P. Wigner, and Edward Teller made up half of the six-member team that directed the Manhattan Project, which created the atomic bomb for the United States during World War II. Teller later became director of the Lawrence Livermore National Laboratory in California, and thought up the Star Wars nuclear defense program as well. In all, between 1905 and 2003, 12 scientists of Hungarian origin won Nobel prizes for scientific research and economic sciences. Two Hungarians also received Nobel prizes in non-scientific areas—Elie Wiesel was awarded the Peace Prize in 1986 and Imre Kertész the Literature Prize in 2002.

Significant Hungarians who emigrated to the United States in the last century include Joseph Pulitzer *(right)*, who rose from a reporter for a German language newspaper in St. Louis to owner of the prominent *New York World*, funded the establishment of the Columbia University School of Journalism, and is memorialized by the Pulitzer Prize for outstanding writers, artists, and journalists; Adolph Zukor produced the first American-made feature film, *The Prisoner of Zenda*, and founded Paramount Pictures Corporation; and William Fox founded the Fox Film Corporation, the forerunner of Twentieth-Century-Fox movie studios.

LIFESTYLE

HUNGARIANS HAVE BEEN MOLDED by the pressures of the past 40 years. Communism promised that people would have to work less, be healthier and happier, and live more comfortably. Instead, they had to work harder, live in small, run-down apartments, and spend most of their free time searching for basic necessities to make life livable.

URBAN LIFESTYLE

Many Hungarians in urban areas live in high-rise apartment complexes called *lakótelep* (LAH-koh-teh-lep). These consist of dozens of ugly, uniform buildings 10 or more stories high and filled with cramped, identical apartments. These developments stand on the edge of towns and often require a long commute to work. But they include markets, shops, bars, and other amenities so that, except for work, it is not really necessary to leave the complex.

Apartments in the *lakótelep* consist of a tiny bedroom for the children that also serves as a study, and a slightly larger bedroom for the parents that is also the living/dining room. The kitchen holds a stove and a fold-out table at which two can sit, and the bathroom is also tiny. Laundry is hung on the balcony or over the tub, and food, towels, kitchenware, and other necessities are stored in closets along the narrow hall.

Newer and more attractive apartments exist, but they are expensive and are targeted at better-paid expatriates. Fancier areas of town hold luxurious homes and villas previously occupied by Party officials. Workers' hostels, usually decrepit domitories for workers at large factories, have largely been sold to private developers or torn down. That, coupled with rising utility prices, has made thousands of people homeless. There are an estimated 30,000 homeless people in Hungary, many of whom line the major streets and subway stations of the capital, begging for spare change.

Above: **Many apartment complexes in the country are old and crumbling. However, with a shortage of housing, no one would even consider refusing an apartment just because it is in a run-down building.**

Opposite: **Hungarians of all ages enjoy spending a day out at the palatial swimming pool in the popular Szechenyi Baths complex in Budapest.**

PLAYING THE APARTMENT GAME

The apartment complexes that ring the edges of all Hungarian and other Eastern European cities and towns are both the achievement and fiasco of the socialist system. Many Hungarians who moved to urban areas to fill the jobs created by industrialization were housed in them, and the monthly rent was just a few dollars. But there were never enough apartments to go around, as the government focused on building new industrial plants and installations. Getting one's own apartment became one of every urban Hungarian's primary goals in life.

After 1990, as part of the privatization process, tenants were offered the chance to purchase their rental apartments and, depending on their income, even to pass them on to children or grand-children. But a housing shortage in Budapest remained, as between 1995 to 1998, only 3,000 new units were built as compared to 15,000 a year between 1971 and 1975. Thus drastic measures were taken with families registering a child at its grandparents' address in order to inherit that apartment when the child grew up; and divorced couples forced to continue living in the same apartment.

With the opening up of the housing market, now that state control is gone, there are more apartments available, but at exorbitant rents. New single-family houses built outside Budapest and other cities have also eased the situation somewhat. But the rising cost of purchasing an apartment means that many young people, even if married, have to save up to 10 years or more for their own home and live with their parents until then. Thus for the majority of urban Hungarians who need cheap housing, playing the "apartment game" will still be necessary for the near future.

The dream of every Hungarian is to have a weekend home where the family can relax.

GARDEN HOUSES

Middle-class Hungarians have been able to find relief from their cramped living conditions at "garden houses" or weekend retreats. The liberalizations of the Kádár government allowed families, after years of saving, to buy a narrow plot of land, usually a fraction of an acre, outside town. Great feats are needed to secure the necessary materials to build, with one's own hands, a tiny house, and many families spend every weekend there, making improvements, cultivating fruits and vegetables, and even processing homegrown grapes into wine.

RURAL LIFESTYLE

In 2000, the Hungarian government completed its 10-year effort to privatize or restitute 80 to 85 percent of the land, leaving only 10 to 15 percent as state land.

Rural living is quite different from that of a *lakótelep* dweller. Hungarian peasants have come a long way since the 1930s; most now live in single-family homes, with a garden attached and a one-acre private plot of land some distance away.

Peasants working after hours in their own gardens and on small private plots have for years produced more than half of Hungary's fruits and vegetables, and a substantial proportion of the livestock as well. Village dwellers are thus able to supply most of their own needs, and are envied by many city residents for what they see as the freer and more bountiful rural lifestyle. On the other hand, most villages lack the cultural and social amenities of the cities, and their social life may be restricted to men gathering to drink in the dark, smoky, and dirty *kocsma* (KOHCH-mah) or bar.

Rural living can be harsh. However, as farmers and peasants grow their own food, they have more control over their lives than city dwellers and do not feel the stress of having to hold more than one job.

GIFTS, FAVORS, AND PATRONAGE

Since many things were not available for purchase during the Communist regime, people grew to rely on friends, relatives, and business associates to make ordinary transactions work. A construction worker might supply some building materials to a Russian teacher who would tutor his daughter in exchange. This system combined elements of a barter economy with the kind of kinship or patron-client relationship found in traditional societies. Sometimes transactions might involve three or four persons, or a favor might be repaid only many months later. But all Hungarians, from the lowliest laborer to the manager of a large factory, learned to be constantly on the lookout for people who could help them, and for ways in which they could assist others. They were always aware of debts and favors owed them in any social situation.

Although goods and services are freely available now, the "favor mentality" has remained strong with Hungarians. They tend to look for ways to beat the system, rather than attaining things directly. This characteristic helps knit people together in their interdependence on each other, but can also turn relations between people into a calculation of cost and benefit.

SOCIAL ATTITUDES

Although most Hungarians hated communism and neither agreed with nor understood its ideology, the cradle-to-grave communist welfare state has left a strong mark on Hungarian attitudes today, especially that of the older generation. They have become accustomed to free health care, guaranteed jobs, and even vacations organized for them by their employers. Thus certain attitudes, such as the expectation that the state will take care of every need, are deeply rooted. As a reaction to communist attempts to regulate their lives, older Hungarians are very protective of their privacy, are suspicious of highly organized group situations, and prefer to spend evenings at home with a few friends than go to a concert or nightclub.

For the generation born in the late 1980s or after, their attitudes reflect a more Western perspective. They hang out with their friends at fast food outlets and other entertainment centers, enjoy rock concerts, and surf the Internet. But at the same time, they are trying to discover and create their own identity. The country's problems do weigh on the minds of Hungarian youths. They have little faith in the political system (although they believe in democracy), lower expectations of what the government has to offer, and they care less for their own community.

CHILDREN, YOUTH, AND FAMILIES

Hungarian families have been getting smaller. The trend is downward, from two children to one child per family, especially in the urban areas. Nevertheless, Hungarians maintain deep bonds with their families. They spend holidays together, send greetings for birthdays and name days, and keep in touch with all the relatives on a regular basis. Children rarely break off contact with parents. Even if family members are no longer on speaking terms, they usually keep informed about each other. Family members are expected to help each other out in getting around the obstacles of daily life and to drop everything to provide necessary assistance in a crisis.

Hungarian families are small, and parents take advantage of dinnertime to impart their wisdom to their children. One of the values closest to the heart of the Hungarian is loyalty to one's family.

Life for children and young people has not been easy. They generally spend many hours in day-care centers and nursery schools. Yet this pattern is changing, at least for affluent families. Hungarian children are dealt with quite strictly and are prepared for hard work and discipline later on. Young people do find time for pleasure, though, whether it is a soccer game in a vacant lot at dusk, a weekend of roughhousing at a crowded public swimming pool, or a romantic walk along the river.

Family life in the countryside is different. Families tend to be larger, and two or three children are the norm. Children spend more time with their families, helping out with chores around the house, in the garden, or in the fields. There is more room to move and relations are more relaxed.

FROM YOUNG PIONEERS TO HUNGARIAN SCOUTS

After the Communists took over Hungary, families were pressured to enroll their children in the Young Pioneers, a kind of communist Scout movement. The Pioneers were gathered together to meet government leaders and visiting dignitaries from other socialist countries and for parades on important communist holidays. After "graduating" from the Pioneers, the next step was entering the Communist Youth League, or KISZ. Membership in KISZ was practically obligatory for young people who wanted to go to college or get job training. KISZ organized summer work camps, weekend outings, concerts, and lectures, but always with an eye to educating and forming young people to fit into the system.

The Federation of Young Democrats (Fidesz) began as an independent alternative to KISZ in colleges and high schools, before becoming a political movement, and finally a party. The Hungarian Scouts Association *(above)* was also reintroduced in 1989, carrying on the traditions of Hungarian Scouting from before World War II, and providing an organized alternative to the discredited Pioneers. Hungarian boys and girls now take part in group activities, such as hiking, swimming, and camping, to develop a sense of community, not just for the sake of conformity. The Hungarian Scouts have renewed their traditional ties with the Catholic Church, and boy and girl Scouts take part in processions and other religious activities.

However, some have charged that the new movement was designed to indoctrinate children with nationalist ideas in the same way that the Pioneers had done with communist ideology. Most families simply prefer to let their children enjoy their leisure time without the supervision of an organization.

PRIDE AND PREJUDICE

Hungarians are extremely proud of their country and that they managed to preserve their traditions through centuries of war, revolution, and foreign domination. This national identity, while inspiring Hungarians to work together to create their new government and economy, has also given rise to a kind of dangerous nationalism that excludes and even victimizes those who are seen as "outsiders" or "enemies." Increasing competition for scarce jobs has also heightened suspicion of foreigners and minority ethnic peoples

The Jews, who once controlled most of the businesses and commerce, have traditionally been the target of prejudice in Hungary. Anti-Semitism has reappeared, in graffiti against the opposition SZDSZ party, in desecrations of Jewish gravestones, and in the writings of populist writer and ultranationalist

politician István Csurka, who believes that Judaism is conspiring with the Americans, the Russians, and the International Monetary Fund to keep Hungary down. But Jews in Hungarian society are well established, very integrated, and able to defend themselves by political or legal means.

The group that is the target of much prejudice are the Roma, who are at the bottom of the social ladder and still lead a mostly separate life from the Magyar majority. They are disadvantaged in the areas of health care, housing, employment, and education, and are blamed for rising crime, violence, and other social problems. Skinhead youths have taken to attacking Roma, along with African and Asian immigrants. Some people from surrounding countries have also been victimized. Nationwide campaigns are now underway to improve relations between Roma and other Hungarian peoples.

In Hungary, like in the rest of Europe, racism and bigotry are making a comeback, and skinhead youths have taken to attacking immigrants and anyone who looks different.

EDUCATION

Since the 1990s, Hungary's education system has been reformed, such as replacing the communist-oriented view of history, politics, and philosophy and the compulsory study of Russian with a broadened, Western-oriented perspective. Private and church-run schools have also reopened.

Free compulsory public education lasts for 12 years and starts at the age of 4 or 5, depending on whether the child attends kindergarten. Students progress from primary (elementary) school to secondary school (high school). After the eighth grade, about 32 percent of students continue at the *gimnázium* (GIM-nah-zee-uhm), or academic high school, and 39 percent go to a vocational high school, where they are trained for mid-level positions in industry, agriculture, trade, or health. Twenty-three percent attend skilled worker training schools. Closely tied to specific industries, these include on-the-job training. The rest join the work force. More than half the graduates of secondary schools attend university or college. Many people go to night school or take correspondence courses while working.

Hungary's education system has produced 14 Nobel Prize winners since 1905. The first Nobel laureate was Philipp E.A. von Lenard for physics in 1905, while the co-recipient of the 2004 Chemistry prize, Avram Hershko, spent his formative years in Hungary before migrating to Israel. Even during the communist years, important advancements were made by Hungarians in the international fields of medicine, physics, and chemistry.

High school students listen to their lecturer in front of the basilica during a field trip to Pécs.

SEX ROLES AND WOMEN'S RIGHTS

In 2000, 45 percent of the workforce was female. But leading positions in government and the economy were still held by men. This gap is closing, with 9 percent of working women in managerial positions in 1999, as compared to 2.2 percent in 1973. Among economically active men, 11.2 percent were in management in 1999 and 5 percent in 1973. Women earn around 78 percent less than men for comparable work because they are often segregated into low level jobs.

The burden of Hungary's transition to a market economy is being borne disproportionately by women. They are the first to be laid off and fall into poverty more often than men do. The child-care system, which used to be free, is losing government funding and can no longer take care of everyone's children.

There is a conservative push to keep women out of the work force. Many Hungarians feel that communism violated their traditional values by forcing women to work. The darker side of the demise of communist "official feminism" is the rise in prostitution and pornography.

Nevertheless, by 2001 female unemployment (5.1 percent) was lower than male unemployment (6.3 percent). There is a gradually changing social climate, with more women working their way to the top. Business ownership is also becoming a career alternative for females in Hungary, women heading two out of every five enterprises established since 1990.

During the communist years, women had the opportunity to train in previously male-dominated technical fields.

RELIGION

HUNGARY'S CHRISTIAN ROOTS reach back a thousand years to the founding of the first Hungarian state and the crowning of King Stephen by the Pope. Since then, religion has been crucial in defining the Hungarian identity, and religious struggles have often been tied up with the struggles of Hungarians to survive. During the communist era, state leaders promoted atheism as the official "religion," and churches, especially the predominant Catholic Church, suffered with the rest of society. As communism faded in the 1980s, religion made a comeback as a symbol of anti-communism and national identity, and church attendance increased. Hungarians today are curious about religion, but it is not an important part of the life of most younger urban Hungarians. Among older people and in rural areas, religion still plays a strong role.

Left: **Roman Catholicism is still a driving force in the lives of older Hungarians. Saint Stephen is the focus of deep veneration. On August 20, Saint Stephen's Day, a grand procession goes through the streets of Budapest.**

Opposite: **The Mátyás Church in Budapest, with its diamond-patterned roof and neo-Gothic spires, is dedicated to the Virgin Mary but is popularly named after the 15th-century king who was married here.**

RELIGION IN HISTORY

Thirteenth-century Saint Erzsébet (Elizabeth) is probably Hungary's most famous saint. She devoted her short life to ministering to the unfortunate and needy, including a colony of lepers she treated with therapeutic mineral waters. She became an object of worship across the Catholic world, and was the subject of paintings by masters Fra Angelico and Hans Holbein the Younger.

The Magyars brought their own well-developed pagan religious ideas with them into the Carpathian Basin. But King Stephen I realized that the adoption of Christianity was essential to the Magyars' long-term survival in Europe. When he chose Western (Roman Catholic) Christianity over the Eastern (Orthodox) variety, his decision put Hungary firmly in the West. Within a few years, Stephen succeeded in converting the whole country to Christianity, by force where necessary. Hungary's later participation in the European religious Crusades against the Ottomans sealed its Christian identity and commitment.

The Protestant movements against the Catholic Church during the Reformation quickly spread to Hungary. The Transylvanian princes who safeguarded some measure of Hungarian autonomy during the more than 150 years of partition between the Ottomans and Habsburgs were mostly Protestants, and Protestantism became identified with the struggle for Hungarian independence against the super-loyal Catholic Habsburgs. Calvinism also became very strong in Hungary, and the eastern Hungarian town of Debrecen became known as the "Calvinist Rome," a center for that denomination of strict, ascetic Protestantism. When the Habsburgs got rid of the Ottomans and became sole rulers of Hungary, they used the Catholic Counter-Reformation movement—a Europe-wide counter-offensive against Protestants—to punish Hungarian desires for independence.

More than two centuries of Habsburg rule succeeded in turning Hungary into a predominantly Catholic country. The attachment to the symbolic crown of St. Stephen proved stronger than opposition to the Habsburgs. The Catholic Church grew into a large landholder and one of the main pillars of economic and political power from the quasi-feudal system of the late 19th century until World War II.

PROTESTANTS AND JEWS

As a result of the Reformation, the majority of Hungarians were Lutheran or Calvinist by the end of the 16th century. But Protestantism was suppressed, and by the 1600s, Hungary was again primarily Catholic. Lutherans in Hungary, despite being in the minority, have contributed much to the country's scholarship, literature, art, science, education, social welfare, and medicine.

The unified Reformed (or Calvinist) Hungarian church was established in 1881. Calvinist priest Gönc Gáspár Károli published the first complete Hungarian-language Bible in 1590, which had a lasting influence on Hungarian intellectual life and literature. Surviving without pastors, teachers, or churches in many parts of the country for much of its early existence, the Reformed church was legalized only in the 19th century.

The first Jews came to Hungary as early as the third century A.D., but most Jews arrived in the late 11th century. Hungary's Jews were divided into two groups. A very religious Orthodox population lived separately in its own communities, following very strict Jewish laws and practices. A less religious group lived in cities and towns, and took up important positions in the economy and later in society. It was this latter group that most enthusiastically accepted the 19th-century proposition to "Magyarize" and were accepted into the nobility. They bought estates and became involved in the government. The Holocaust in Hungary wiped out most of the Jewish communities outside Budapest.

Hungary has the largest Jewish community in Eastern Europe, with between 90,000 and 150,000 practicing the faith.

79

Although the Communist regime introduced its own ceremonies to replace the Christian ones, people still went to church for baptisms, weddings, and funerals.

COMMUNIST ATHEISM

Communist ideology saw religion as a false promise of heavenly justice that could lead people away from the struggle for real communist justice. In addition, the church in Hungary had been a firm supporter of the old order. Thus the existence of a strong church and widespread religious beliefs could not be allowed to exist under the communist system. The communists nationalized church institutions and property, and many religious organizations were banned. In 1951, the State Office for Church Affairs was set up to control religious life.

Cardinal Joseph Mindszenty, the highest Catholic official in Hungary, was imprisoned in 1949. He was released by rebels during the 1956 Revolution and took refuge in the American Embassy in Budapest, where he remained until his departure from Hungary in 1971, a lone symbol of opposition to communism until his death in 1975 in Austria.

The communists developed their own rites and ceremonies to replace those traditionally offered by the Church: a Pioneer initiation ceremony took the place of baptism and Communion, and a state ceremony was required for all marriages. A communist funeral ceremony was also developed, though it was not forced on people and it never caught on. Especially after the Stalinist era, when the campaign against the church was relaxed, Hungarians resumed baptisms and church marriages (in addition to the civil wedding). The churches reached an accommodation with the communist rulers, in which they were allowed to operate without harassment and even received a certain amount of state support, in exchange for accepting the supreme authority of the Party and the permanency of the communist system. But, by this time, Hungarians, not the most religious people in the first place, had lost interest in religion, and church attendance did not rise beyond a small portion of the population.

SAINT STEPHEN AND HIS CROWN

One of the first things the new freely elected Parliament did in 1990 was to restore Hungary's traditional coat-of-arms. This national symbol—called a *címer* (TSEE-mehr) in Hungarian—is also known as the Lesser Coat of Arms, and was determined by a Royal Order in 1874 and confirmed in 1895 and 1916.

The *címer* is topped by the crown of St. Stephen, the symbol of Hungarian nationhood. The bottom right side contains a silver patriarchal cross coming out of a gold coronet. This "apostolic" double-cross became the sign of King Stephen I, representing the religious authority bestowed upon him by Pope Sylvester II and his mission to convert the pagan Hungarians to Christianity.

Born a pagan in the village of Esztergom, Prince Stephen was baptized at the age of 10. King Stephen was zealous for the conversion of his people to Christianity, establishing episcopal sees and monasteries, such as the Benedictine Abbey of Pannonhalma and the center of the Hungarian Catholic Church in Esztergom. Christianity was established as the state religion and pagan practices were severely punished. Every tenth town was required to build a church, furnished by the king himself, and to support a priest. King Stephen himself used to distribute alms to the poor in person, occasionally in disguise.

RELIGIOUS REVIVAL AND NATIONAL IDENTITY

As the communist system fell apart in the 1980s, people turned to the church for new ideas. But because of the willingness of Hungarian church authorities in the past to compromise with the Communists, the church in Hungary received much less respect and played a much smaller role in the breakdown of the communist system than in Poland, Romania, East Germany, or Czechoslovakia.

Where religion did play a big role, and continues to do so, is on the symbolic level. The Christian religion has long been tied to the idea of Hungarian national independence through the Holy Crown of St. Stephen. So the crosses that many young people wore in the late 1980s symbolized not only the rejection of communist atheism, but also loyalty to the Hungarian nation and its independence. The MDF party successfully used religious symbolism to present itself as the truest representative of Hungarian values and win the 1990 elections.

Surveys in the late 1990s showed that only 15 percent of those surveyed considered themselves to be religiously active. The majority, 55 percent, said that they practiced religion in their own way or were only nominally religious. Approximately 30 percent said that they were nonreligious.

The government allows the free practice of religion. In 2002 the government paid the main religious groups 5.64 billion HUF as compensation for the assets confiscated during the Communist regime.

Hungary now recognizes more than 50 different religions, meaning that they get a level of state funding based on their size. These include, in addition to the main religions (Roman Catholic, Calvinist, Lutheran, and Jewish), religions not traditionally found in Hungary, such as Buddhism (arriving in 1960) and Islam.

Islam was recognized in Hungary in 1916 but was later banned by the government in 1949. In 1988 Muslims renewed their activities. Eastern Orthodox churches have maintained a presence in Hungary since the 10th century. There are now about 40,000 Orthodox Christians in Hungary, including Serbian, Romanian, Hungarian Orthodox, and Bulgarian Orthodox. The Jehovah's Witnesses and the Hare Krishnas have been considered "socially destructive," accused of separating young people from their families but their presence is tolerated. The new interest in all things foreign has brought a number of more unusual religions to Hungary. Hungarians will continue to experiment with offbeat religions, as with other trends, until they tire of their new freedom to do so.

Although Christianity *(opposite)* **is still the main religion, several new religious groups have begun to appear on the streets of Budapest, including the Hare Krishnas** *(below)*.

LANGUAGE

THE HUNGARIAN LANGUAGE is unique and sounds strange to the untrained ear. Hungarians are proud of the uniqueness of their language, and it forms a major part of their identity. Hungarian is difficult to learn, and few foreigners make the effort, so Hungarians have always had to use other languages—Latin, German, Russian, and English—to communicate with the outside world.

THE UNIQUE MAGYAR TONGUE

The native Uralic language (the Finno-Ugric branch) brought by the Magyar tribes was later influenced by the Turkic language spoken by the Turkish Ottoman Empire that ruled most of Hungary in the 16th and 17th centuries. Several hundred words, mostly related to farming, were borrowed from the agricultural Slavic tribes that the Magyars themselves conquered when they occupied the Carpathian Basin. Further influences were provided later by Slovakian, Serbian, and the other surrounding Slavic languages, as well as by Latin, French, and—on the force of the several hundred years of domination by the Austrian Habsburg Empire—German. But despite all of these pressures and influences, the basic character of the Hungarian language remained unique and unchanged. Hungarian today is a linguistic island: a language of Asian origin molded by European history.

CONTRIBUTIONS TO ENGLISH Hungarians pride themselves on their language's contributions to English. These include *coach* (in the more commonly British sense of bus or carriage) from the Hungarian *kocsi* (KOH-chee), which itself is a derivative of Kocs, the town where a special kind of horse-drawn vehicle was made. Paprika and husar (from the Hungarian *huszár*, a light calvary soldier) are other contributions.

A couple chats on a park bench by a lake.

THE CHARACTER OF THE LANGUAGE

Hungarian is an agglutinative language, meaning that easily recognizable word stems are expanded by adding prefixes and suffixes to create expressive compound words. There are no pronouns; relationships such as *in*, *on*, *at*, and *around* are expressed by suffixes, as are possession and the identity of the subject, or the object of the sentence.

Another confusing aspect is word order. Hungarians tend to start their sentences with the things they feel need to be emphasized most at that particular moment. This is very flexible. It is as if the sentence "John gave Mary the cat" could just as well be "John the cat gave Mary," or even "Gave John Mary the cat." Hungarians know whether a word is a subject or an object by its suffix, not by its place in the sentence.

The Hungarian language also makes no distinction between male and female. The pronoun *ő* stands for *he* and *she*. But this does not mean that Hungarian is less "sexist" than other languages. Any woman holding an occupation or position must be identified by adding *nő* (woman) to the title (e.g. *tanárnő*, from *tanár* and *nő*, teacher-woman).

THE LANGUAGE OF MANY VOWELS

The Hungarian language has more vowels than almost any other—14 in all. These consist of seven "short" vowels, *a, e, i, o, u, ö, ü*, and their long forms *á, é, í, ó, ű, ő*, and *ú*. What looks like an accent mark, however, does not denote syllable stress or a slightly altered pronunciation like in French or Spanish, but is in fact a completely different letter. The long *á*, for example, is listed separately in the dictionary from *a*, and pronouncing or writing one instead of the other is likely to create a completely different word. This is one thing that makes Hungarian especially hard for foreigners, since mispronouncing or switching a short vowel with a long one will result in a blank stare from a Hungarian. What sounds like a minor shift to a foreigner is, to a native speaker, a completely different sound, and therefore word.

LANGUAGE AND NATIONALITY

In the early 19th century, a developing class of intellectuals made writing and speaking in Hungarian a national campaign. In parliament in 1825, during a discussion to encourage the growth of the Hungarian language and culture, young Count István Széchenyi took to the floor and speaking in Hungarian, offered to found a Hungarian Academy of Sciences to advance the cause. By the late 19th century the joint efforts of poets and politicians had established Hungarian as the dominant language.

The Hungarian language became the definer of Hungarian nationality. In order to secure a Hungarian majority in the territory, Hungarian nationality was offered to anyone who would adopt the language. Thus, to this day, a "true Hungarian" is defined in terms of allegiance to the Magyar tongue as one's first and primary language. Hungarians tend to be very concerned that their language be spoken and written "correctly."

Hungarian has eight dialects, with two spoken outside Hungary's borders, all mutually understandable. Hungarians living in a Transylvanian village may speak an "older" form of Hungarian, but it will still be immediately understood by someone from Budapest.

In the past, the Hungarian ruling classes preferred to speak Latin, German, or French. Many had only a crude knowledge of their native tongue, or none at all.

Hungarian names are said in reverse, with the family name first and the given name second. Thus the great composer is really called Bartók Béla, and the former prime minister Antall József. A formal title comes at the very end: Dr. John Smith would thus be Smith John Doktor (or, to be very formal, Doktor úr). Foreign names are generally spoken in the "normal," Western order.

GREETINGS

Hungarians are very formal and proper in their relations with each other. In pre-Communist times, numerous titles and corresponding forms of address were used to define exactly the ranking of all of society, from the king right down to the lowliest peasant serf. During the Communist period, the old forms of address were abolished in favor of the universal *elvtárs* (EHLV-tarsh), or comrade.

Hungarians address any adult by the formal *ön*, until or unless invited to use the informal *te*. But neighbors will often use the formal form with each other for years. Married people generally address their in-laws formally for the rest of their lives. Younger adults are less formal with each other, and tend to use the *te* form without hesitation. But when in doubt, Hungarians always choose the formal version, to avoid embarrassment or insult. An older form of the formal address, *maga* (MAH-gah), can sometimes be heard, but it is also used as an insult.

MINORITY LANGUAGES

Although there are educational opportunities available in minority languages (German, Slovakian, and Romanian), members of these groups often speak Hungarian better than they do their "native" tongue. Still, street and shop signs are found in these second languages in villages that have a large proportion of minorities.

The Roma form the biggest linguistic minority in Hungary, but those speaking solely the Roma language, Romany (a relative of ancient Sanskrit, brought from the Roma's original home, which was India) make up only one-third of the group. In the 18th century, the Roma were not allowed to use Romany, but had to learn Hungarian. But since 1998, Romany has been taught in schools to a majority of Roma students.

FROM RUSSIAN TO ENGLISH

During the communist period, learning Russian was made compulsory for all Hungarian schoolchildren starting in the fifth grade. A student who continued to high school would end up having studied Russian for eight years or more, but he or she was proud to have forgotten most of the language of the Soviet occupiers within a few short years after leaving school.

In 1990, the new government abolished the compulsory study of Russian in schools, and now students may choose any of a number of Western languages instead.

Hungarians are now eager to learn Western European languages, especially English and German. Knowledge of these two languages will help them conduct business in the international arena and adapt to Western culture.

Private language schools, with names like "London Language Studio" or "Boston Language School," have sprung up all over the capital and can be found in many smaller towns as well. Many young Hungarians can speak English and are eager to practice the language whenever they get the opportunity. Older people are more likely to know German. If you know Russian, you might still be able to converse with one or two former high officials or the rare lover of Russian culture.

Posters targeted at trendy young people are now as likely to be written in English or German as in Hungarian.

ARTS

THE ARTS IN HUNGARY have a long tradition of confronting the country's two constant problems: the lack of national independence and the absence of social justice. For centuries, the arts—especially literature—have played a major role in social movements and, at key points in Hungarian history, have been the spark that set off revolutions.

The transition to a free market system has brought sudden changes that have proved very confusing to Hungarian artists. State subsidies are being cut drastically, and artists, musicians, and writers must quickly learn how to be commercially successful in order to survive. At the same time, the fall of Communism has deprived creative artists of a target for their protests and satirizations. Without state funding, the arts in Hungary today are in a financial and creative crisis.

Left: **The change to a free market economy has resulted in a proliferation of street artists and musicians. They now have to learn how to make a living from their artistic talent.**

Opposite: **Hungarian folk dancers perform at a local festival.**

LITERATURE AND THE NATION

The best-known examples of early Hungarian literature are the *Gesta Hungarorum*—chronicles of a monk, known only as "Anonymus," which told the story of the Magyars' migration, settlement, and development up to around A.D. 1200—along with the work of the first great Hungarian poet, Janus Pannonius, the star of King Matthias Corvinus's 15th-century court.

Hungarians are avid readers and the bookseller's kiosk is a familiar sight on Budapest streetcorners.

The first major poet to write verse in Hungarian instead of Latin was Bálint Balassi, who started a tradition of lyric poetry in the 16th century. He died defending the holy city of Esztergom from the Ottomans. In occupied Hungary during the 16th and 17th centuries, poets kept the nation's spirit alive by bringing news from fortress to fortress.

The two centuries of Habsburg rule were a setback for Hungarian literature, because educated Hungarians then spent most of their time abroad. But in 1784 the proposal by Habsburg Emperor Joseph I to make German the official language of the nation, spurred a new wave of literary rebellion. Writers such as Ferenc Kazinczy, who rejuvenated the language with modern words, József Katona, whose *Bánk bán* (Regent Bank) qualifies as the first great Hungarian drama, and poet Ferenc Kölcsey, whose *Himnusz* (Hymn) became the Hungarian national anthem, all focused on improving and glorifying the Hungarian language in the service of national unity. The Revolutionary Era of 1848 produced Hungary's most beloved poet, Sándor Petőfi.

INNOVATION AND CONFLICT

The 20th century saw a new phase in Hungarian writing with Endre Ady's *New Poems*. He combined modernist ideas with traditional national values. The result was a strange yet beautiful style of writing and controversial ideas on politics, that opposed war and the oppression of peasants.

Writers flocked to Paris and other European capitals to sample the new, avant-garde creative movements of impressionism, expressionism, modernism, and (later) dadaism. The literary focus shifted from traditional settings in the countryside to Budapest. A new, cosmopolitan style befitting a modern European capital developed. Its flagship was the journal *Nyugat* (West), which was a potpourri of poetry, short stories, serialized novels, essays, news, political commentary, and translations of foreign literature.

After World War I, a group of young writers and students started exploring conditions in the countryside, looking for "the real Hungary." What they found was appalling poverty. Out of this "village explorers movement" came the populist movement, which has remained a major force in Hungarian literature to this day. Gyula Illyés produced probably the finest example of these writings, *People of the Puszta*. The populists' city counterparts were the urbanists—the cosmopolitan writers of Budapest, who took the city and the whole world as their subject, and who grouped around the *Nyugat* and other journals. One urbanist who achieved immortality in Hungarian literature was the tragic poet Attila József.

During the creative years of communism, well-known writers included György Konrád and Péter Esterházy, and László Nagy and István Vas were known for their poetry. Post-1989 poets include János Térey, Krisztián Peer, and Dániel Varró, while András Cserna-Szabó is noted for his short stories. In 2002, Imre Kertész became the first Hungarian to be awarded the Nobel Prize for Literature.

The writers of the interwar era did much of their work—and carried on most of their debates —in Budapest coffee houses, mostly in the Café New York. This continued a long tradition—Sándor Petofi had, after all, proclaimed his 1848 revolutionary demands in such a café. After the fall of Communism, the New York, which had been renamed the Hungaria, regained its old name and again became a center for literary life —as well as a tourist attraction for intellectuals.

TIVADAR CSONTVÁRY KOSZTKA AND HUNGARIAN PAINTING

Hungarian painting has been much less important than literature in the development of the nation, and has gained much less international recognition than Hungary's musicians and composers. Hungary's history of foreign occupation made it difficult for artists to find the support they needed to develop a characteristic national style. When a demand arose for paintings in the 19th century, Hungarian artists did little more than imitate the styles current in Vienna or France, especially classicism. At most, they took Hungarian historical events or personalities for their subjects. Mihály Munkácsy was probably the most renowned of these 19th-century painters, although he spent most of his creative life in Paris. The prolific post-impressionist painting of József Rippl-Rónai at the end of the last century brought Hungarian art up to the most advanced current styles.

In 1881 a young pharmacist in the southern Hungarian town of Pécs experienced a vision. God appeared before him and told him to go to the ends of the earth and paint the spiritual wonders he saw. Tivadar Csontváry Kosztka set off to fulfill this destiny. The paintings he produced in the next few years show mystical and religious subjects *(above, Mary's Well in Nazareth)*, strange and symbolic figures, and seductive colors, often painted on huge canvasses. Csontváry painted wondrous scenes from Sicily, Lebanon, Jerusalem, Switzerland, and the Hungarian *puszta*. His paintings all exhibit the painful gap between his mad, holy visions and the desolate reality of human life that he saw. Although his work has been classified as expressionist, it shows signs of primitivism and naturalism, and even of the future trends of art nouveau and surrealism.

Csontváry's genius was little recognized during his wandering lifetime. He was "discovered" in the 1920s, after his death, and again in the 1950s. In recent years, his paintings have become extremely popular among younger Hungarians. Prints of Csontváry's paintings, such as *Solitary White Cedar* or *Pilgrimage to the Cedars of Lebanon*, gracing the wall of a Hungarian *lakótelep* apartment, represent the romantic hopes and often difficult reality of such apartment dwellers.

FROM LISZT TO LIGETI

Hungarian music is a product of two traditions: the mainstream classical European tradition, and a unique, "Asian" type of native music. The Rákóczi Rebellion of the 18th century generated a characteristic form, the *kuruc* song, which was passed on from one generation to the next.

Franz (Ferenc) Liszt, perhaps Hungary's most famous pianist and composer, masterfully married European Romanticism with native musical traditions. He consistently used Hungarian themes, both musical and historical, in his compositions. Born in 1811 of a Hungarian father and an Austrian mother, Liszt got his musical education in Vienna and spent much time in Germany and Italy.

Zoltán Kodály and Béla Bartók were heirs of Liszt's legacy. Kodály, Hungary's favorite composer, devoted himself to general music education. His persistent advocacy of making

It is fitting that this school choir should perform in front of a portrait of Zoltán Kodály, a man who devoted himself to the musical education of Hungarians.

music available to all helped spread an appreciation of music to all Hungarians. Since Kodály, Hungarian music has been characterized by competent and prolific productions of standard classical works, based around such institutions as the Liszt Ferenc Music Academy, the Budapest Philharmonic, the Hungarian Radio Choir, and the Franz Liszt Chamber Orchestra. The isolation of the Stalinist years and the general discouragement of innovation have caused the greatest names in Hungarian music since Kodály, such as György Ligeti, to emigrate and make their careers abroad.

BÉLA BARTÓK (1881–1945), A HUNGARIAN ORIGINAL

Classical and modernist composer Béla Bartók, together with his colleague Zoltán Kodály, spent his summers traveling to small villages and rural settlements to collect samples of genuine folk melodies. They asked village elders to sing the songs they remembered and recorded the results on wax cylinders. Their efforts saved the vanishing native musical traditions. Today, over 100,000 different recordings are classified and preserved in the archives of the Hungarian Academy of Sciences.

Bartók, like Kodály, saw native melodies as the deepest expression of the "true Hungarian soul." He incorporated his Hungarian collections—as well as those he made of the melodies of neighboring Slovakians, Romanians, Bulgarians, and Turks—into his compositions, which ranged from folk songs to dissonant modernist experiments. Unlike Kodály's, Bartók's music never became a favorite of Hungarian listeners; it is often difficult and strange. But pieces such as his *Mikrokosmos* for the piano, his piano quartets, and his later *Concerto for Orchestra* are considered masterpieces of precision, innovation, and individuality. Bartók died in exile in New York in 1945, poor and lonely.

Bartók's role in Hungarian culture did not end with his death. His music was banned in Hungary during the 1950s, and young people played his records as an act of political opposition. Later, in the 1970s, his name came into use by populists as an adjective expressing pure interest in peasant art: as in a *bartóki* person, or even *bartókiság*, "Bartók-ness." His memory was rehabilitated by the reform-minded late Kádár regime. His portrait was put on the 1,000-forint note, and one of the three state radio stations is called Bartók Radio (the other two are named after Lajos Kossuth and Sándor Petőfi)—elevating him to equal status with the greatest national heroes.

In 1988 negotiations between the Hungarian government and Bartók's two sons resulted in the return of his remains to Budapest for reburial. The body was brought by ship from New York to England and then by motorcade across France, Germany, and Austria, with concerts at major towns along the way. The event dominated the Hungarian media for weeks, and the essentially apolitical composer was celebrated all at once as a populist, an urbanist, an antifascist, an advocate for minority rights, a national hero—and, almost as an afterthought, as a musician.

COMMUNISM AND CULTURE

The arts in Hungary in the early 1950s were dominated by "socialist realism," meaning that all art had to reflect the reality of the "socialist person." Short stories and novels told of workers or peasants overcoming doubts and learning to work harder for communism, eventually joining the Party and vowing to work even harder in the future. Paintings and sculpture likewise turned to depictions of strong, self-sacrificing, heroic workers holding the communist flag high. Even in poetry and music, odes to Soviet leader Joseph Stalin, or to Hungarian leader Rákosi, were preferred. Some writers were able to preserve their integrity by writing "for the desk drawer"—works that could not possibly be published at the time, but that might be able to appear in the future if the system ever changed.

The Kádár era was one of compromise and liberalization. Much more was allowed to be published, produced, and shown than previously, although there were certain very firm limits. No criticism of the Soviet Union or the Soviet-Hungarian alliance was allowed, nor of the socialist system or of the leading role of the Communist Party in political life. Private matters, such as love, death, and family life, were free territory, and social problems could even be brought up if done carefully. Writers learned the limits of what was allowed and began to restrain themselves to avoid the risk of crossing the line and being persecuted.

The 1960s and 1970s produced a new wave of art, exploring the conditions of life for the majority of Hungarians. Prominent examples were studies by György Konrád, a sociologist who later became a novelist and political essayist, and by Miklós Haraszti, a dissident activist, lecturer, and former member of Parliament for SZDSZ. There was a blossoming of novels, short stories, poetry, and all other kinds of writing, on themes personal and historical, and sometimes somewhat political.

A love poem was allowed to be published only if the hero discovered that the struggle for communism was more important than personal happiness.

"READING BETWEEN THE LINES"

Communist rulers tried to control the cultural arena through an extensive and thorough system of censorship that was firmly established by the beginning of the 1950s. All newspapers, magazines, articles, books, plays, films, works of art, and even songs had to be approved by Party authorities before they could be presented to the public. To pass censorship, the work had to have a communist political view, fit the form prescribed by socialist realism, and not offend any powerful leaders. Artistic and political persons who fell out of grace became "non-persons," and could not be referred to by anyone by name.

This system of censorship softened in Hungary during the Kádár era, and by the late 1960s, there was no longer any prescreening of written work. (Theater, film, and music still had to be approved in advance.) But direct opposition to the system was still not permitted, and it was left to editors to be responsible for the invisible lines that should not be crossed, or risk losing their jobs. Writers especially, and other artists too, developed a sense of what they could safely write and produce, and what would go too far—in short, they became their own censors.

One way to avoid the problem of self-censorship was a style of allegory that became known as "reading between the lines." Creative artists adopting this style used a seemingly innocent setting—an incident from the past, from another country, or both—in such a way that a clever reader or audience knew that the moral or political lesson of the work was to be applied to the current situation in Hungary. The Revolution of 1848 was a favorite early subject, allowing writers such as Gyula Illyés to indirectly advocate a fight for national independence. Later, the soccer field became a common setting; Miklós Mészöly's *Death of an Athlete* caused a scandal, and Antal Végh's story *Why is Hungarian Soccer Sick?* was actually withdrawn from the market within days of its appearance—apparently the lines to be read between were a little too wide. Géza Ottlik's *School at the Frontier,* set in a pre-World War II military school, showed the ominous effects of the over-disciplining of youth; others used insane asylums or other institutions to spin dramas of the individual's relationship to society.

Hungarian theater was subject to the strictest control from the very beginning of the communist era, because of the theater's potential for subversion. But hard as it tried, the state was unable to ensure that socialist realism ruled the stage, and plays in particular were used to transmit hidden political messages. Such details as the scenery or costuming of a familiar and seemingly safe work could tip the audience off that another meaning was intended. Thus the staging of Shakespeare's *Hamlet* caused a major scandal in 1952, and a lesser one some 10 years later, as the director subtly but unmistakably referred back to the earlier scandal. László Németh's 1953 play, *Galilei* (about the late Renaissance Italian scientist), was performed for the first time just days before the outbreak of the 1956 Revolution, contributing to the upheaval. Clever artists and audiences found that even works by genuine communists like the German playwright Bertolt Brecht could be turned against the corrupt communists of the Kádár era.

THE FILM INDUSTRY

After 1958, the Hungarian film industry was reorganized and, surprisingly, given a large amount of freedom to explore new and critical themes. Miklós Jancsó, one of Hungary's greatest directors, made *The Round Up* in 1965, about Hungarian peasants forced to act as collaborators and traitors during the 1848 Revolution, a theme that paralleled the humiliation of the peasantry in the 1950s. The Stalinist years became a frequent topic, whether of critical dramas, cutting farces, or hard-hitting documentaries.

Márta Mészáros is a fine director who deserves greater international recognition.

In the 1980s the financial plight of the state studios forced them to enter into coproduction agreements with West European studios. István Szabó, Hungary's most prominent director, used this situation to make films that were both seen by international audiences and implicitly critical of his country's political system. An example is the Oscar-winning *Mephisto*, about a German artist who sells his soul to the Nazis— an easily understood parable about the compromises made by his fellow Hungarian artists under Kádár.

A distinction of the Hungarian film industry is the prominent role of women directors, of whom Márta Mészáros is the best-known, in making documentaries and dramas that deal especially with the problems of women in Hungarian society. Since 1989, a new wave of directors have emerged, such as Kornél Munruczó, György Pálfi, and Benedek Fliegarf.

An outdoor concert in Hungary.

FROM POP TO PROTEST

The first rock music in Hungary came in the early 1960s as more or less a direct import from the West translated into Hungarian. Lyrics tended toward standard love themes; a few songs touching on politics or human rights were banned.

By the late 1970s, new influences were reaching Hungary from the West in the form of reggae, punk, rap, and heavy metal. The same problems that fostered these movements in the West—inflation, poor employment prospects, housing shortages, and general alienation from society—showed up in Hungary too, only with a more intense hopelessness. There was an explosion of new groups, and their music was angry, outrageous, and opposed to the system.

Some groups tried experimental forms of music, but others adopted sexist, racist (anti-Roma or anti-immigrant), or even fascist/Nazi themes, using extremely violent and profane language and images in their songs and performances. Their popularity has continued, expressing the radical mood of some young people in the country.

TRADITIONAL ARTS AND CRAFTS

The most characteristic craft forms are embroidery, pottery, and carving. Elaborate embroidery, featuring flowers, leaves, birds, and spiral designs, was traditionally required for the peasant bride's dowry, which might include a dozen ornate pillows and embroidered sheets, two to four decorated feather quilts, and six to eight elaborate tablecloths.

Sárköz in Transdanubia, the Matyó region in the Great Plain, and Kalocsa on the southern Danube are especially well-known for their needlework. The Székely people in eastern Transylvania use hides and sheepskins to make thick coats and jackets, which are then elaborately decorated.

Leatherwork and intricate horn carving is the domain of the men of the *puszta*, who produce canes, whip handles, pen knives, flutes, and pipes, featuring everyday scenes and patriotic symbols. The old plains style of ceramics produces pottery smoked black in the kiln, unglazed and varnished with pebbles. Standard, mass-produced clothes and furnishings have now replaced traditional styles in Hungarian peasant homes, but festivals and special occasions still bring out characteristic costumes.

Embroidery by Hungarian peasant women is some of the finest in Eastern Europe. Embroidered tablecloths and clothing can now be bought from Transylvanian peasants in Budapest and from stalls at holiday craft fairs.

There has been an enormous influx of foreign movies since the opening up of the economy.

CRISIS IN THE ARTS

The advent of a free market system after 1990 was a shock to creative artists. Not only did they now have to worry about the commercial side of their art, but a massive influx of cultural products from the West—everything from reality television programs to the *Harry Potter* novels and the latest Brad Pitt flick—has flooded the market and made it even more difficult for Hungarian artistic productions to compete. This crisis has hit the film industry particularly hard. Although a few films are still being made with foreign investment and some government subsidies, many film technicians and other personnel have been thrown out of work.

The positive side of the change is, of course, the possibility for the Hungarian arts to finally express themselves in complete freedom, without self-censorship or fear. Furthermore, many feel that now creative artists can return to universal themes and pure artistic achievement, thus making Hungarian culture meaningful for all the world. Others, however, wonder whether high quality can be sustained when the artist has to constantly worry about survival. And some even see signs of old habits—state manipulation of the media and self-censorship, now in fear of nationalist rather than Communist taboos—returning, leaving the Hungarian arts stuck between two worlds, without the freedom of capitalism or the material support of Communism.

THE BUDAPEST *SZOBORPARK*

After the fall of communism, many Hungarians wanted to remove all traces of the hated system from their everyday life. The statues put up by the Communists were an obvious target, and plans were made to put all of the capital's communist monuments in a statue park (*Szoborpark*). But the task of cutting down and removing these massive figures of granite and bronze proved to be more difficult, and far more costly, than anyone thought. Many people complained that, in a time of increasing hardship, the money should be used for more pressing social needs.

There were also philosophical and political disputes. Some argued that the symbols of 40 years of oppression should be "wiped off the face of the earth." Others felt that they had become a basic and inseparable part of the city's landscape and should be left to stand, along with monuments from previous eras. Russia protested at the "desecration" of memorials to Red Army soldiers who fell on Hungarian soil during World War II. It was charged that the removal of a statue of the 1919 revolutionary Béla Kun was in effect a tribute to the repressive Horthy regime that drove Kun out. One group of veterans of the 1956 uprising got so carried away that they toppled a statue of the Greek goddess Nike because the five-pointed star she carried resembled the communist red star.

After three years of debate and preparation, the sculpture park opened in the spring of 1993. It holds 42 prime examples of socialist realist sculpture from all over Budapest on a 20-acre (8-hectare) expanse. Huge figures of Marx and Lenin, of the traditional socialist worker-hero, of Soviet soldiers, and of obscure Hungarian Communists now have only one another to intimidate. The effect is strange, and can hardly be described as "artistic," but is most definitely a first.

LEISURE

HUNGARIAN LIFE HAS BEEN CHARACTERIZED more than anything by the lack of leisure time. An emphasis on work and the pressures of survival under communism left little time and energy for entertainment or fun. When they did have a chance, Hungarians tended to react to their burdensome and over-organized lives by retreating to the privacy of family and home life. Younger Hungarians are now more likely to take the initiative to go to rock concerts and organize trips or sports activities. But middle-aged or older Hungarians still tend to be worn out or in poor health, seeking their comfort in television and from the bottle.

Opposite: **A good soak at a health spa and a mentally challenging game of chess with friends—two favorite pastimes of Hungarians. Some of the world's greatest chess players are from Hungary.**

Below: **Senior citizens can afford to spend their time playing cards in the park with their pals.**

Street parties during the Budapest Parade are a recent phenomenon.

COMMUNISM AND LEISURE

Communist leaders in the early years tried to organize and direct the leisure time of the people. There was the "mass song" movement of singing of folk song-like odes to communism, as well as organized dance troupes and hiking excursions. A "House of Culture" was set up in every village and every district of the larger towns, and offered a constant flow of programs designed to educate and mold rather than to entertain. Vacations were dedicated to work camps or educational retreats. Those who chose to organize their own leisure activities were seen as suspicious loners.

In the 1960s people's private lives were given back to them, as long as they did not use them to oppose the system. There were still obligatory marches on official holidays and some extra work, but people could and did take the chance to spend time with family and relatives, to celebrate special occasions at home, to relax with music or television, or to attend cultural events.

Vacations were also freed for relaxation; most workers took advantage of the very cheap packages offered by the businesses where they worked or their official trade union, which operated hotels at lakes and other recreation spots all over the country.

With the economic crisis in the 1970s through to the post-communist years, it became common for Hungarians, especially men with families, to take on second and even third jobs to be able to buy a weekend house or a car, or just to survive. After putting in a normal work day at an "official" job, he spent the evening moonlighting at a second job, or plying his official trade for private customers. Weekends were also typically spent working, and vacations from the first job were a prime opportunity to make even more by working at the extra jobs. Thus many worked practically nonstop, their only respite being a drink, which could be had on or off the job. Women worked just as hard between a full-time job and taking care of all the usual family responsibilities.

Young Hungarians, like young people everywhere, are very resourceful and especially in recent years, have been able to plan their own leisure time and recreation. Even during communist times, travel regulations were lenient. Thus many young people took trips to Western European countries. These contacts with the West brought new styles and activities to Hungary, and young people began to organize alternative festivals, gatherings, concerts, and events. Even the communist Houses of Culture were opened up for yoga classes, jazz concerts, lectures on the environment, and self-help groups. And young lovers needed no one's permission to go for a romantic stroll in the park or along the river.

With the fall of the communist government, leisure is no longer as regulated as it once was and more kinds of activities are readily available.

THE HOUSE-RAISING PARTY

One feature of rural living is the *kaláka* (KAH-lah-kah) or house-raising party. Like the traditional American barn-raising, extended family members and even the whole village would come together to help a family build a new house. This old tradition gained a new usefulness in the Communist era, when material shortages and the necessity to use personal connections to get goods made this type of cooperation necessary for any large building project. It even spread to the city: young people wishing to bypass the years-long waiting list for an apartment of their own would enlist all of their friends and colleagues to provide whatever help they could on weekends and vacations—often lasting many months—to build their own place. Although it is now possible to simply pay to have a house built if one has the money, a bit of the *kaláka* tradition still survives.

SPAS AND BATHS

Hungary has more than 1,000 thermal springs, some with a temperature higher than 86°F (30°C). Early Celtic and Roman settlements have been found near springs. The ruins of the Roman regional capital, located outside Budapest, are called Aquincum, from the Celtic *Ak-Ink*, meaning lots of water. The splendid Roman baths were fed by a system of canals and had floor and wall heating. The Magyars also recognized the therapeutic potential of the waters. But it was the Turks who fully harnessed the land's thermal powers and left behind the network that exists today.

Hungary uses about 200 million cubic yards (153 billion cubic m) a year of thermal waters. Thermal treatments include drinking the water and bathing in natural caves, pools, lakes, and elaborately constructed spas. Spas in special locations are recommended for specific ailments, whether arthritis, open wounds, or lung problems. There are even radioactive mud cures. Tourists have flocked to Hungary from as far back as the 17th century to take the cures, and many Hungarian town names are recognizable as former or current spa locations by the suffix *fürdő* or *füred*, meaning bath. The thermal lake at Hévíz is the world's second largest natural hot spa, with a surface area of more than 470,000 square feet (43,664 square m), but this wonder was once threatened by bauxite mining (for Hungary's important aluminum industry), which had siphoned off half of the water nature previously pumped in and nearly destroyed both the lake's healing heat and its ecological balance. Fortunately, bauxite mining in the area has ceased.

The majestic baths of Budapest are meeting places as well as places to relax and ease the day's aches and pains. They used to be meeting places for lovers, but strict separation of the sexes since Turkish times put a stop to that. At baths where mixed crowds are allowed, bathing suits must be worn. Otherwise, small "aprons" are handed out to cover the essentials. At some baths, chess players concentrate on boards fixed at the level of the water. One may also want to get a massage or just relax in the steam, or sit and admire the splendid architecture of the spa buildings, which range in style from Turkish to classical to art nouveau.

Fencing requires agility and great concentration. Hungarian fencers are among the best in the world.

SOCCER AND OTHER SPORTS

Hungarians are avid sports fans, and membership in sports clubs and associations is very high: nearly 650,000 registered competitors in over 3,200 sports associations. Fans avidly read several sports newspapers in order to keep up-to-date on sports stars' contract negotiations, family life, and coaching changes, in addition to their scores and standings.

Soccer is the favorite sport in Hungary. Fans follow both the national league and international matches. Although the level of league play is not as high as in the larger European countries, Hungary's national teams did very well in the past. Older fans can still recite from memory the names of the players on the legendary national "Golden Team" of the early 1950s. The successes of the "Golden Team" gave Hungarians hope that, though their political and social aspirations were suppressed at home, at least in sport they could achieve greatness. Hungarians also closely follow developments in swimming, water polo, gymnastics, canoeing/kayaking, and fencing, as well as team hand-ball, penthathlon, cycling, sport shooting, and basketball, and in winter, ice hockey, skating, and cross-country skiing. Hungarians are also proud of the chess-playing Polgar sisters, two of whom are grandmasters of the men's events.

HUNGARY AND THE OLYMPIC GAMES

Hungary's successes in Olympic competition (mainly in the summer sports) are a source of great national pride. Despite its small size, Hungary has won 10 or more gold medals in seven Olympic Games since 1936. The total medal haul between 1894 and 2004 was 458, including 156 gold medals, more than either Australia or Canada. Each time the games come around, the country is gripped by the Olympic fever, and headlines across the press celebrate each Hungarian gold medal.

Hungarian Olympic athletes have been especially proficient in modern pentathlon, fencing, gymnastics, wrestling, and water sports. Hungary's swimmers have impressed the world and Krisztina Egerszegi *(below)* and Tamas Darnyi have become national heroes, respectively winning 5 and 4 gold medals between 1988 and 1996. The Hungarian water polo team has taken the gold medal an amazing eight times, and the soccer team won it three times. The modern pentathlon, combining horse riding, fencing, shooting, swimming, and running, is said to present a similar challenge to that faced by Magyar warriors in times past.

Hungary was one of the founding nations of the modern Olympic movement in 1894, and the country has participated in every game since the beginning, with the exception of the 1920 Olympics, when the destruction wrought by World War I and political instability prevented it, and the 1984 Los Angeles Games, when Hungary's political leadership forced its athletes to follow the Soviet-led boycott, disappointing the country greatly. Following the tragic events of 1956 just three weeks before, Hungarian athletes stoically appeared at the 1956 Melbourne Games and the country placed fourth in the overall medal standing. A measure of national pride was salvaged in the semifinal round of the water polo competition, when Hungary defeated the Soviet Union 4-0 in a game called off early to prevent rioting and fought so hard that the water was said to have turned red from the wounds the players inflicted on each other. The Hungarian team went on to win the gold without losing a single match.

Many Hungarians compete in the Olympics as citizens of other countries. For example, Romanian gymnast Ekaterina Szabo, who won four Olympic golds in 1984, was an ethnic Hungarian from Transylvania—yet another point of pride for Hungarians.

"HIGH" AND "LOW" CULTURE

Cultural performances are relatively cheap: movie tickets cost US$2–4, opera performances cost less than US$35, and theater tickets can cost as little as US$5. The theater season lasts from September to June. In the summer there are a number of festivals around the country, offering both Hungarian and international or experimental theater. Excellent classical music and opera performances can be seen all year round, and the Budapest Spring Festival, which has expanded to include other major cities, draws many foreign visitors as well. Small, "alternative" movie houses and film clubs still abound in Budapest. They cater to students and young people, showing older, "oppositional" Hungarian and other Eastern European films, as well as art films and independent productions from the West.

All that Dance is a moving ballet danced to the music of Franz Liszt and Carl Orff. Here, it is performed at the State Opera in Budapest.

Most Hungarians stay home to watch television and videos, watching on average about four hours of TV a day. Viewers can choose from many local broadcast and satellite channels, such as *RTL Klub, TV2, Duna Television, Magyar Televízío* and *M2*. In addition, many have satellite antennas that also receive international and European channels in German, English, and Hungarian, such as *Animal Planet Europe, Extreme Sports Channel, HBO Hungary*, and *Fox Kids*.

Hungarians are avid readers and post-communism bookstores and the stalls of street vendors have been flooded with books of all variety, such as horror fiction, pornography, self-help books, science fiction, and romance novels from the west. With their formerly well-protected monopolies gone, the traditional book publishers face stiff competition from many new private publishing houses.

FESTIVALS

HUNGARY'S TRADITIONAL HOLIDAYS AND FESTIVALS were based on the religious and agricultural calendars, including saints' days, and planting and harvest days. The communist system substituted the traditional holidays with "political" holidays marking landmarks in communist history. Few believed in these new holidays, but all were forced to recognize and "celebrate" them. With the new post-communist system, these unpopular holidays have been abolished, and the old traditional ones have been returned to their former importance.

BIRTHDAYS AND NAME DAYS

While birthdays are celebrated in Hungary, they are not nearly as important as "name days." The days on the Hungarian calendar are each assigned to a certain Christian name that is commonly known and used. These assigned days are based on religious traditions, historical events, or birthdays of famous people, so that every name has a name day. In fact, the most common Hungarian names, such as László, Zoltán, or Zsuzsanna, each have two or even three days assigned to them—Maria has eight! In that case, one of these days is chosen for the child of that name, and family and friends are told to celebrate on that day and not the others. On name days for the most common names, flower-sellers do a fabulous business, and it seems that every second person on the street or subway has a bouquet in hand.

Name days in Hungary are first of all a family occasion. Fellow students or co-workers give flowers and a greeting, and in the evening the lucky Ágnes or János goes home to assembled family members, more flowers, a special dinner, and toasts. Small gifts may be given by the immediate family, but coming together to celebrate is more important. Birthdays are celebrated in a similar way, but with a smaller gathering, and are usually not marked at all by friends or colleagues.

Opposite: **Hussars in traditional costumes ride in the center of Budapest as part of Hungary's March 15 national day celebrations, commemorating the failed 1848 anti-Habsburg revolution.**

Below: **Traditional dress is a regular feature of wine festivals.**

COMMUNIST AND "OPPOSITION" HOLIDAYS

Communist holidays in Hungary marked days important to the Soviet Union and the founding of the Hungarian Communist state. The major ones were April 4, Liberation Day, the date in 1945 when the Soviet Red Army expelled the Nazis and gained control of the whole country; May 1, International Workers' Day; August 20, Constitution Day, the date of the inauguration of the Hungarian communist state in 1949; and November 7, commemorating the Russian Bolshevik Revolution of 1917. All of these days were public holidays, filled with official parades, meetings, and festivities that workers and students were pressured to attend.

The communists also tried to take over days that were traditionally important to Hungarians to make them "revolutionary" without being too "nationalist." Thus, on March 15, the anniversary of the outbreak of the 1848 Revolution, there would be an official ceremony, which in later years even featured national symbols like the national red, white, and green tricolor flag. In schools the date was coupled with the communist holidays of March 21, commemorating the 1919 Béla Kun Revolution, and April 4,

HOLIDAYS IN HUNGARY

New Year's Day	January 1
March 15 National Day (1848 Revolution)	March 15
Easter Monday	March/April
Labor Day	May 1
Pentecost (Whit Monday)	May/June
St. Stephen's Day/First National Day	August 20
October 23 National Day (1956 Revolution)	October 23
Christmas	December 25–26

to become "Revolutionary Youth Days," featuring readings of patriotic and revolutionary poems, visits by political figures, and other programs. The point was to recognize these national days enough to convince the people that the communist system respected their values, but not so much that communist holidays would be upstaged or people encouraged to further acts of patriotic nationalism.

Despite these efforts, opponents of the communist system were still able to make national days, especially March 15, into occasions for opposition demonstrations. Demonstrators would meet at an "unapproved" place, for example at the Petőfi statue in Budapest instead of in front of the National

Communist parades required the participation of thousands of young people and involved massive displays of military might, as much to impress the West as to subdue the local population.

Museum, which was the site of the official ceremonies. They would then march to other squares or statues of patriotic importance, chanting slogans or even handing out leaflets. These occasions were attended by a few hundred people, and often resulted in clashes with police. The demonstrators gradually succeeded in changing the meaning of that date into something threatening to the regime. By the end of the 1980s, days connected with the 1956 Revolution, which had been completely taboo under Kádár— October 23, the day the revolution broke out, and June 16, the execution of 1956 Prime Minister Imre Nagy—also began to be marked by opposition demonstrations. The transformation of the calendar became complete with the fall of the communist system and the reinstatement of traditional national holidays.

FOOD

HUNGARIAN FOOD is hearty and rich, meaty and high in cholesterol. Paprika and goulash have become symbols of Hungarian cuisine. The country's food reflects not only its own nomadic Asiatic Magyar past but also Turkish, Jewish, Serbian, Austro-German, and American influences.

THE PEPPER

The characteristic ingredient in Hungarian cooking is paprika, which finds its way into almost every Hungarian dish. We know paprika as a spice, the ground, dried red pepper that gives a characteristic flavor and reddish color to most Hungarian dishes. But Hungarians also use the word for any fresh pepper, from the "white paprika," through yellow and red, to the small dark red peppers that set the mouth on fire. Fresh peppers are either sweet or hot. The taste, along with the shape and color, guide the shopper in making a selection. Several different types, as well as the ubiquitous powdered form, can appear in one dish, such as *lecsó* (LEH-choh), a common stewed mixture of peppers, tomatoes, and onions, often including sausage or bacon and sometimes scrambled with eggs.

Paprika appeared in Hungary around the 16th or 17th century. At first, it was used only by the lower classes, who could not afford the "genuine" spices imported from the Far East. But it gradually worked its way up the social ladder and, by the middle of the 19th century, became an essential part of Hungarian cuisine. Ever since, paprika has been considered a typically and uniquely Hungarian spice. The pepper helped Hungarian scientist Albert von Szent-Györgyi Nagyrapolt win the Nobel Prize in physiology or medicine in 1937 when he discovered vitamin C in one of its richest sources—paprika.

Paprika is an important ingredient in Hungarian cooking as evidenced by hanging peppers in a market *(above)* **and the variety at a produce stall in Budapest's Central Market** *(opposite).* **Paprika comes in many shapes and sizes, as well as different degrees of spiciness.**

Goulash cooking on an open fire at the International Children's Meeting in the summer of 1993.

SOUPS AND STEWS

Hungary's culinary claim to fame, goulash (*gulyás*, GOO-yash, in Hungarian), although known abroad as a stew, is actually more common in Hungary as a soup. The dish is cooked with mutton, beef, or pork, and there is even one variation called *hamis* (HAH-mish, fake) with no meat at all. Goulash supposedly dates back to the time of the original Magyar tribes, who cooked meat together with onions and then dried the product to carry with them on their marauding expeditions. The dish was reconstituted later—the world's first "instant" soup. Later, goulash was traditionally cooked in a special copper or cast-iron kettle called a *bogrács* (BOH-grahch), hung from a stick over an open fire. (The dish might still be served in a restaurant in a mini-*bogrács* over a flame.)

However, the dish we know as goulash is more like the various Hungarian stews that go by the name of *pörkölt* (PUR-kult) and *paprikás* (PAH-pree-kash). These consist of any meat (pork, beef, chicken, lamb, veal, or—a Hungarian traditional specialty—wild boar), occasionally with mushrooms or potatoes, stewed in fat with onions and lots of paprika, and served over small dumplings called *galuska* (GAH-loosh-kah). A *paprikás* is distinguished by the addition of sour cream, which makes it thicker and richer. Side vegetable dishes served with it include spinach, green peas, or cabbage, either stewed or creamed.

A full Hungarian meal almost always begins with a soup of a lighter variety, such as mushroom, cauliflower, or green pea. These soups are made by briefly frying the main vegetable together with a few pieces of carrot and parsley, adding water and later a roux (soup thickener) made from oil, onion, flour, and paprika, and finally a pasta called *tarhonya* (TAR-hone-yah), made of flour and egg dough. Other options for the soup course are meat broth made from either beef or chicken, and a Hungarian specialty, cold fruit soup, made from cherries or plums and milk or sour cream. Other Hungarian soups, including *halászlé* (HAL-ahss-lee, fish soup), *bableves* (BAHB-leh-vesh, bean soup), and goulash itself, are substantial enough to be a meal in themselves, and are not usually followed by another main course.

THE ORIGINS OF THE BÉCSISZELET

The *bécsiszelet* (BAY-tseeh-seh-leht), or *wiener schnitzel* in Austria, is a tenderized veal cutlet, coated with an egg-and-bread-crumb batter and fried, usually served with potatoes or mixed salad. It is well-known in Hungary but has controversial origins. Some say that it is a traditional Hungarian meal, others say that it was born in Vienna, veal being the great specialty of Austrian cuisine. Still others say that it began life in Milan and was later brought to the Habsburg empire, a culinary melting pot from which the classical dishes of the modern-day Austrian cuisine emerged.

One story starts in Italy with Austrian General Radetsky and his cook. Radetsky was at war with the Italians, trying to suppress the First Italian War of Independence (1848-49). While in Italy, his cook learned local technique of breading meat.

This, the Italians, apparently learned from the Spanish, who learned it from the Moors, who learnt it from the Arabs. When the war was over, Radetsky's cook taught this technique to the cook of Franz Joseph I, Emperor of Austria and later King of Hungary. This was how the *bécsiszelet* came to Hungary. In its original form, it was made from veal cutlets and fried in butter. The Hungarians later made it from pork and fried it in pork lard.

DRINKING AND TOASTING TRADITIONS

The frond-like objects hanging from the rope across the front of this house are wine-tasting gourds. They are used to take wine out of the barrel to fill glasses.

Hungary's national drink is a clear brandy called *pálinka* (PAH-lin-kah), which can be made from apricots, pears, cherries, plums, grape skins, or a mixture of fruits—to be sampled at one's own risk! Hungarian hosts offer the drink to guests or visitors at any time of the day or evening, and it is rude to refuse without a good reason. *Pálinka* is best served cold and is drunk straight from a shotglass (a shot is a single measure, usually an ounce), in one gulp if possible. *Házi* (HAH-zee, or homemade) *pálinka*, made by a farmer rather than in a distillery, is especially prized. It may sometimes be replaced by vodka, which Hungarians believe to be a cure for an upset stomach, and is drunk in the same way. The fashion for all things Western

POLITICAL DISHES

Some typical Hungarian foods have made their way into the international political vocabulary, as apt descriptions of unique phenomena in the country's political history. Thus there was the first postwar communist leader Rákosi's "salami tactics," by which he gradually dismantled all of the competing non-communist political parties, first by "slicing off" a piece (declaring certain leaders to be "reactionaries" and expelling them from political life), then another, and another, until there was no party left. And the political system that developed during the Kádár era is typically known as "goulash communism," meaning a form of market economy working within the frame of a socialist economy, ensuring "a goulash in every *bogrács*."

has brought gin, French brandy, and whiskey into many Hungarian shops and homes, but *pálinka* remains the hard liquor of choice for the true Hungarian.

Two Hungarian wines have achieved international renown. *Egri Bikavér* (AIG-ree BEE-kah-vair), "Bull's Blood of Eger," is a dark and strong wine from that northeastern valley. *Tokaji* (TOH-kah-yee), the sweet white dessert wine made from grapes around Tokaj, along the Tisza River farther east, has been called "the wine of kings and the king of wines" for its prominence at royal tables over the centuries. The quality, cost, and sweetness of the best *tokaji*, the Aszú variety, is indicated by the number of *puttonyos* (POO-tohn-yohsh) it contains. A *puttonyos* is a basket that measures the amount of a paste made from the region's withered, super-sweet grapes. Other fine Hungarian wines, both red and white, are made around Lake Balaton, along the southernmost stretch of the Danube, and near the towns of Pécs and Sopron.

Learning the Hungarian toast—*Egészségére* (EH-gayse-shay-gay-reh), meaning to your health—is often a foreign visitor's initiation into the mysteries of the Hungarian language. With this toast, glasses are then clinked and drained. When drinking beer, however, this was not the custom for 150 years. Legend has it that the Austrians who executed the freedom-fighting Hungarian generals of the 1848 Revolution clinked beer glasses as the fatal shots rang out. Only in 1999 did Hungarians start clinking beer glasses again.

Hungarian wines, such as the "bull's blood of Eger" *(center)*, **bring out the full flavor of goose liver pâté, salami, and other Hungarian specialties.**

125

The *piac* is a veritable treasure trove of fresh vegetables and fruits. This is where most Hungarians do their grocery shopping because it offers the lowest prices.

SHOPPING AND DINING HABITS

Hungarians like to buy their foods fresh, doing most of their shopping at the *piac* (PEE-ahts), or market. It might be a vast indoor market hall, an outdoor brick-walled enclosure, or just a designated open space, filled by rows of sellers of vegetables, fruits, eggs, cheese, meat, and fish. The sellers are sometimes the growers of the food themselves, but more often they buy produce directly from the grower. Some stalls offer a wide variety of fruits and vegetables, along with a few packaged products; others are filled with mounds of potatoes, peppers, or melons, which they offer for the best price and sell steadily. Elderly women offering a few carrots, onions, or turnips from their gardens fill the spaces in between stalls. The shopper brings a bag, and the seller, after weighing out the requested quantity—usually by putting metal weights on a manual scale—dumps the produce into the shopper's bag, right on top of what is already there.

The *piac*—which is closed on Sunday and Saturday afternoon—is a lively place. Sellers praise their wares, shoppers debate whether they really got the firmest tomatoes or the freshest mushrooms, and there is often a beer stand or two full of thirsty customers, and all kinds of non-food items are hawked around the outskirts. Western, mainly Austrian and German, chains are opening more and more super-markets in Hungarian cities and towns. Having a wider and more appetizing selection than Hungarian supermarkets, they are especially popular with those who have more money to spend and less time to search the *piac* for the best bargains. But since fruit and vegetable stands can be found even near bus stops and at busy streetcorners, and most families have little storage space in their refrigerators, shopping often and buying fresh are still the norm.

Most Hungarians rarely go to restaurants, except on very special occasions, such as weddings or the annual office celebration. They prefer to eat at home and go out only for pastry and coffee, or for a drink.

The midday meal is traditionally the main meal and is generally eaten at work or school, in a cafeteria or company canteen. Supper may be a soup, leftovers, or cold meats, served with cheese, bread, tomatoes, and peppers. Weekend midday meals and evening suppers with guests usually involve the preparation of several courses. The table setting is informal, and the company may eat in more than one sitting if there are too many guests for the small table. Good manners are still expected when eating, and small children (or sloppy adults) are quickly reprimanded if they eat loudly or carelessly.

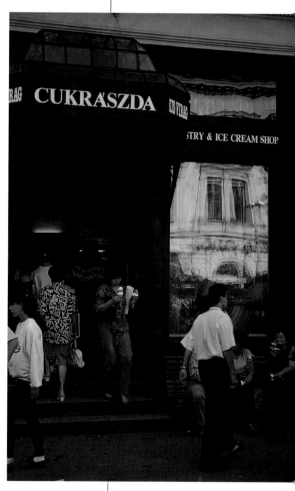

This pastry shop also sells ice cream, which is eaten as a special treat.

Row upon row of pastries and sweets entice the customer in the *cukrászda*.

CAKES, PASTRIES, AND SWEETS

The Hungarian *cukrászda* (TSOO-krahs-dah), or pastry shop, is a palace of wonders, filled with creamy delicacies like *Rigó Jancsi* (REE-goh-yahn-chee), a chocolate-flavored jelly roll sandwiched with chocolate custard and cream, or *gesztenye püré* (GEH-stehn-yeh PYU-rai), a chestnut puree with whipped cream. Poppy seeds feature in many different Hungarian confections—from pastries and bread pudding to noodles eaten with poppy seeds and sugar. Coffee (*kávé*) was first brought to Hungary by the Turks. Served espresso-style—often in a café called *presszó* (PRESS-soh)—it is drunk with milk, cream, whipped cream, or sugar.

Another characteristic Hungarian delight, and a favorite of children, is *palacsinta* (PAH-lah-chin-tah), a rolled crepe filled with jam, chocolate powder, syrup, cottage cheese, or sweetened nuts, or else an elaborate mixture of several of these. (There is also a savory variety, filled with *pörkölt* or cabbage.) *Palacsinta* is not available in bakeries, but at special stands in resorts, parks, and other places where Hungarians go to relax.

FAST FOOD, HEALTH FOOD, AND THE HUNGARIAN DIET

Political changes and the influx of Western businesses, habits, and tastes have begun to affect the Hungarian diet. Traditional kinds of "fast food," including *lángos* (LAHNG-gohsh, a plate-size piece of deep-fried dough made from potatoes and topped with salt, garlic, sour cream, and grated cheese), sausage, corn-on-the-cob, and fried fish, have been around for years, later augmented by *hamburgerek* and *hotdogok* (hamburgers and hot dogs). But the arrival of McDonald's, followed by a host of other American chains with their flashy advertisements, English-language signs, and shiny outlets, has introduced a new generation of Hungarians to the international "fast food culture." These are not the cheapest places to eat; one meal in a fast food restaurant costs more than a meal in most traditional restaurants. A recent survey showed that only a third of Hungarians have ever visited such a fast food place. Those who eat there regularly tend to be young and affluent urban Hungarians, many of whom use these places to meet their friends.

A trend that has been slower to spread to Hungary is the "health food" craze, with its concern about cholesterol, fat, and meat intake. Hungarian cuisine can be spectacularly unhealthy, featuring pork in high proportions, *töpörtyu* (TUH-pur-tchew, pork cracklings), *szalonna* (SAH-lohn-nah, Hungarian bacon eaten straight or with bread), and *zsír* (ZHEER, pork lard used for everything from frying onions for stews and soups to baking cakes and pastries or spreading directly on bread). These are only mildly balanced by the traditional "salads," which for Hungarians mean pickles, pickled cabbage or peppers, or perhaps sliced tomatoes. Vegetables, if they do appear, are either breaded and fried or cooked almost beyond recognition in a *főzelék* (FUH-zeh-layk, vegetable stew). In addition, the more exotic portions of animals—like pigs' knuckles, liver, kidney, tongue, cow stomach lining, bone marrow, calf's brain, chicken gizzards, or items called simply "inside parts"—are prized delicacies. The first health food stores, vegetarian restaurants, and muesli cereal could be seen in the capital by the late 1980s, but these fashions have not caught on with Hungarians, and the places that remain are more likely to cater to health-conscious tourists. However, some individually-minded younger Hungarians have become committed vegetarians or, at least, healthier eaters, and there are signs that such new ideas are slowly making their way into Hungary's food consciousness.

BIBLIOGRAPHY

Central Intelligence Agency World Factbook. www.cia.gov/cia/publications/factbook/geos/hu.html#Intro

Crampton, R.J. *Eastern Europe in the Twentieth Century and After.* London and New York: Routledge, 1997.

Csáki, György and Gábor Karsai. *Evolution of the Hungarian Economy 1848-2000, Volume III: Hungary From Transition to Integration.* New York: East European Monographs/Columbia University Press, 2002.

Fallon, Steve and Neal Bedford. *Lonely Planet: Hungary.* Victoria: Lonely Planet Publications, 2003.

Gergely, Anikó and Ruprecht Stempell. *Culinaria Hungary.* Cologne: Könemann, 2000.

Ministry of Foreign Affairs of the Republic of Hungary. *Fact Sheets on Hungary.* Budapest: Pharma Press, 2000-2003.

Molnár, Éva. (editor). *Hungary: Essential Facts, Figures and Pictures.* Budapest: Hungarian News Agency Corporation, 2001.

Padányi, Ágnes. *Hungary: Step by Step.* Budapest: Hungarian National Tourist Office, 2003.

Richardson, Dan and Charles Hebbert. *The Rough Guide to Hungary* (Fifth edition). London: Rough Guides, 2002.

Wakeman, Rosemary. (editor). *Themes in Modern European History since 1945.* London and New York: Routledge, 2003.

Wegs, J. Robert and Robert Ladrech. *Europe Since 1945: A Concise History.* New York: St. Martin's Press, 1996.

INDEX

FAST FOOD, HEALTH FOOD, AND THE HUNGARIAN DIET

Political changes and the influx of Western businesses, habits, and tastes have begun to affect the Hungarian diet. Traditional kinds of "fast food," including *lángos* (LAHNG-gohsh, a plate-size piece of deep-fried dough made from potatoes and topped with salt, garlic, sour cream, and grated cheese), sausage, corn-on-the-cob, and fried fish, have been around for years, later augmented by *hamburgerek* and *hotdogok* (hamburgers and hot dogs). But the arrival of McDonald's, followed by a host of other American chains with their flashy advertisements, English-language signs, and shiny outlets, has introduced a new generation of Hungarians to the international "fast food culture." These are not the cheapest places to eat; one meal in a fast food restaurant costs more than a meal in most traditional restaurants. A recent survey showed that only a third of Hungarians have ever visited such a fast food place. Those who eat there regularly tend to be young and affluent urban Hungarians, many of whom use these places to meet their friends.

A trend that has been slower to spread to Hungary is the "health food" craze, with its concern about cholesterol, fat, and meat intake. Hungarian cuisine can be spectacularly unhealthy, featuring pork in high proportions, *töpörtyu* (TUH-pur-tchew, pork cracklings), *szalonna* (SAH-lohn-nah, Hungarian bacon eaten straight or with bread), and *zsír* (ZHEER, pork lard used for everything from frying onions for stews and soups to baking cakes and pastries or spreading directly on bread). These are only mildly balanced by the traditional "salads," which for Hungarians mean pickles, pickled cabbage or peppers, or perhaps sliced tomatoes. Vegetables, if they do appear, are either breaded and fried or cooked almost beyond recognition in a *főzelék* (FUH-zeh-layk, vegetable stew). In addition, the more exotic portions of animals—like pigs' knuckles, liver, kidney, tongue, cow stomach lining, bone marrow, calf's brain, chicken gizzards, or items called simply "inside parts"—are prized delicacies. The first health food stores, vegetarian restaurants, and muesli cereal could be seen in the capital by the late 1980s, but these fashions have not caught on with Hungarians, and the places that remain are more likely to cater to health-conscious tourists. However, some individually-minded younger Hungarians have become committed vegetarians or, at least, healthier eaters, and there are signs that such new ideas are slowly making their way into Hungary's food consciousness.

GULYÁSLEVES (GOULASH SOUP)

In Hungary, *gulyásleves* (GOOH-yaash-leh-vehsh) is served with fresh white bread or dumplings, dried hot paprika pods, and *kadarka*, or red wine.

   In restaurants, *gulyásleves* is often served in small kettles as a reminder of its origins, when it was cooked, often by men, in the open in kettles over a wood fire.

1¼ pounds (600 g) beef (neck or shoulder)
1 large onion, peeled and finely chopped
3 tablespoons vegetable oil
½ teaspoon caraway
1 clove of garlic, crushed
Ground paprika (sweet)
Salt to taste
1 medium carrot, diced
1 medium parsley root, diced
1 medium tomato, quartered
2 bell peppers, seeded and chopped
2 stalks celery, including leaves
14 ounces (400 g) potatoes, peeled and chopped
Pasta pieces

Cut the meat into ¾-inch (2-cm) cubes. Heat the oil in a large pot (12-cup/3-liter capacity), then cook the onions until translucent. Add the caraway and crushed garlic, and cook briefly. Remove from the heat, then add the ground paprika and the meat, and season with salt. Cover with a lid and leave to cook gently, adding a little water if necessary. When the meat is half cooked, add the carrot, parsley root, tomato, bell peppers, and celery. Pour in 6½ cups (1.5 liters) water, and simmer gently for 15 to 20 minutes. Add the potatoes. When the meat and potatoes are cooked, add the pasta pieces. Cook for another 5 minutes. Serve hot.

MEGGYES PISKÓTA (SPONGE CAKE WITH MORELLO CHERRIES)

Meggyes piskóta (MEH-dyesh PEEHSH-kooh-tah) is a traditional sponge cake that uses the dark red cherries grown in Hungary's orchards. Other dark red cherries, such as bing cherries, may be used in place of morello cherries.

1 pound (500 g) pitted morello cherries
⅔ cup (150 g) butter
1⅓ cups (150 g) confectioners' sugar
4 eggs, separated
1⅔ cups (180 g) flour

1 teaspoon baking powder
⅓ cup (50 g) confectioners' sugar
2 teaspoons vanilla sugar
Butter and flour for the pan or tin

Rinse the cherries and drain in a sieve. Cream the butter and confectioners' sugar together, then beat in the egg yolks. Sift the flour and baking powder together, then gradually fold into the egg mixture. Whisk the egg whites until stiff, and fold loosely into the batter. Butter a jelly-roll pan and dust with flour. Spread the batter over the pan and scatter the cherries on top. Bake in a preheated (400°F/200°C) oven for 30 minutes. (Do not open the oven door for the first 5 minutes.) Prick the cake with a skewer or toothpick to test whether it is done. Turn off the oven and leave the cake to cool in the oven with the door open. When the cake has cooled, dust it with a mixture of confectioners' sugar and vanilla sugar, and cut into squares.

ECONOMIC HUNGARY

Natural Resources
- Mining
- Oil Refinery
- Timber

Agriculture
- Crops
- Fishery
- Fruits
- Livestock
- Vegetables
- Vineyards

Services
- Airport
- Port
- Tourism

Manufacturing
- Heavy Industry
- Light Industry
- Processed Foods
- Textiles
- Vehicles

ABOUT THE ECONOMY

OVERVIEW
Hungary has made big strides in transforming from a centrally-planned economy into one of the most advanced market economies in Central Europe. Unemployment and inflation rates have fallen, but average incomes and the average standard of living remains low.

GROSS DOMESTIC PRODUCT (GDP)
US$139.7 billion (2003 estimate)

GDP SECTORS
Services 67.3 percent, industry 28.4 percent, agriculture 4.3 percent (2001 estimate)

INFLATION RATE
4.7 percent (2003 estimate)

LAND AREA
93,030 sq km

LABOR FORCE
4.2 million (1997 estimate)

CURRENCY
Hungarian forint (HUF)
Notes: 200; 500; 1,000; 2,000; 5,000; 10,000; and 20,000 forint. Coins: 1, 2, 5, 10, 20, 50, and 100 forint.
USD 1 = 200.273 HUF (October 2004)

LABOR FORCE BY OCCUPATION
Services 65 percent, industry 27 percent, agriculture 8 percent (1996 estimate)

UNEMPLOYMENT RATE
6.1 percent (2003 estimate)

LAND USE
Agriculture 6.5 percent, industry 33.7 percent, other sectors 59.7 percent (2000 estimate)

AGRICULTURAL PRODUCTS
Wheat, corn, sunflower seed, potatoes, sugar beets, pigs, cattle, poultry, dairy products

INDUSTRIES
Mining, metallurgy, construction materials, processed foods, textiles, chemicals (especially pharmaceuticals), motor vehicles

MAJOR EXPORTS
Machinery and equipment, other manufactures, food products, raw materials, fuels and electricity

MAJOR IMPORTS
Machinery and equipment, other manufactures, fuels and electricity, food products, raw materials

MAJOR TRADE PARTNERS
Austria, China, France, Germany, Italy, Japan, Russia, the Netherlands, UK, and the United States

PORTS AND HARBORS
Budapest, Dunaújváros

GLOSSARY

bejgli *(BAY-glee)*
A rolled Christmas pastry filled with poppy seeds or walnuts.

busójárás (BOO-shoh-yah-rahsh)
The Busójárás Festival celebrates the last day before the start of Lent and the end of winter.

címer (TSEE-mehr)
Hungary's coat-of-arms.

csikós (CHEE-kohsh)
Hungarian cowboy.

collectivization
The process by which the Communist government forced private farmers off their land and into large communal farms.

Communism
A political philosophy asserting that everyone should be equal and should work together for the common good.

cukrászda (TSOO-krahs-dah)
A pastry shop that sells ice cream and coffee too.

feudal landholding
A system in which the land the peasant works does not belong to him completely. His right to own the land depends on his landlord or another person.

gimnázium (GIM-nah-zee-uhm)
Academic high school.

kaláka (KAH-lah-kah)
Villagers getting together to build a house.

lakótelep (LAH-koh-teh-lep)
A high-rise apartment complex.

Magyars
Ethnic Hungarians.

nationalism
The feeling that people of one's own country or ethnic group are better than others.

nomenklatura
A class of privileged Communist Party officials.

pálinka (PAH-lin-kah)
Brandy made from pear, apricot, or cherry.

piac (PEE-ahts)
A fruit and vegetable market, or flea market.

populism
The 1930s political movement trying to improve conditions of the peasantry.

proletariat
Industrial working class.

puszta (POO-stah)
Hungarian plain.

virsli (VEER-shlee)
Pork sausages.

FURTHER INFORMATION

BOOKS

Atkinson, Catherine and Trish Davies. *From Stroganov to Strudel: Great Traditional Cooking from Germany, Austria, Hungary, and the Czech Republic.* London: Southwater, 2000.

Banffy, Miklós. *The Writing on the Wall: the Transylvanian Trilogy. Book I: They Were Counted.* London: Arcadia, 1999.

Brahms, Johannes. *Schirmer's Library of Musical Classics: Hungarian Dances.* New York: G. Schirmer, 1994.

Denes, Magda. *Castles Burning : A Child's Life in War.* New York: Simon & Schuster, 1998.

Dohnanyi, Erno. *Complete Rhapsodies and Other Works for Solo Piano.* New York: Dover, 1999.

Kontler, Laszlo. *A History of Hungary: Millennium in Central Europe.* Hampshire and New York: Palgrave Macmillan, 2003.

Popescu, Julian. *Major World Nations: Hungary.* Philadelphia: Chelsea House Publishers, 2000.

Smith, Danny. *Lost Hero: Raoul Wallenberg's Dramatic Quest to Save the Jews of Hungary.* London: HarperCollins, 2001.

WEBSITES

Centreurope. www.centreurope.org/portailgb/top10/hungary-links.htm

EU Business. www.eubusiness.com/topics/Hungary

Activities of the European Union: Partnership for the accession of Hungary.
http://europa.eu.int/scadplus/leg/en/lvb/e40103.htm

Hungarotips. www.hungarotips.com

Hungary Factbook 2000. www.factbook.net/hungary/economy.php

Hungary.hu Government Portal. www.magyarorszag.hu/angol/orszaginfo/alapadatok/alapadatok_a.html

Hungarian National Tourist Office. www.hungarytourism.hu

International Monetary Fund. www.imf.org/external/country/HUN

Ministry of Foreign Affairs Republic of Hungary. www.mfa.gov.hu/Kulugyminiszterium/EN

Panoramas.hu. www.panoramas.hu

The Regional Environmental Center Country Office: Hungary. www.rec.hu/e_index.html

FILM

Super Cities: Budapest. International Video Network, 1995. (VHS)

Maniura, Peter (director and producer). *Sir Georg Solti: the Making of a Maestro.* Image Entertainment, 2001. (DVD)

Szabó, István. *Mephisto.* Anchor Bay Entertainment, 2001. (DVD)

BIBLIOGRAPHY

Central Intelligence Agency World Factbook. www.cia.gov/cia/publications/factbook/geos/hu.html#Intro

Crampton, R.J. *Eastern Europe in the Twentieth Century and After.* London and New York: Routledge, 1997.

Csáki, György and Gábor Karsai. *Evolution of the Hungarian Economy 1848-2000, Volume III: Hungary From Transition to Integration.* New York: East European Monographs/Columbia University Press, 2002.

Fallon, Steve and Neal Bedford. *Lonely Planet: Hungary.* Victoria: Lonely Planet Publications, 2003.

Gergely, Anikó and Ruprecht Stempell. *Culinaria Hungary.* Cologne: Könemann, 2000.

Ministry of Foreign Affairs of the Republic of Hungary. *Fact Sheets on Hungary.* Budapest: Pharma Press, 2000-2003.

Molnár, Éva. (editor). *Hungary: Essential Facts, Figures and Pictures.* Budapest: Hungarian News Agency Corporation, 2001.

Padányi, Ágnes. *Hungary: Step by Step.* Budapest: Hungarian National Tourist Office, 2003.

Richardson, Dan and Charles Hebbert. *The Rough Guide to Hungary* (Fifth edition). London: Rough Guides, 2002.

Wakeman, Rosemary. (editor). *Themes in Modern European History since 1945.* London and New York: Routledge, 2003.

Wegs, J. Robert and Robert Ladrech. *Europe Since 1945: A Concise History.* New York: St. Martin's Press, 1996.

INDEX